PRAISE F
SAVING MY LI

"My good friend, Dan Laizure, has written a great book. It is a very personal look into Dan's life. The purpose of the book is to share what he has learned so we can benefit from his experience. There is a wealth of insight contained in this courageous look at life.

Dan tells his story in an honest, unflinching style. There are very few of us who care to look honestly at our lives, and even fewer with the guts to share our story with others. Telling the story is only part of the value of this book. The author's main purpose is to share nine lessons he has learned that will help each of us live better lives.

This book made me reflect on my own life. Which, of course, is its purpose. One thing it made me think about is how lucky I am to be able to call Dan Laizure my friend. He is a smart, insightful, and generous man. His book is ultimately a gift of his generosity."

—Dr. Ron Wilkins

SAVING MY LIBRARY

SAVING MY LIBRARY

NINE LIFE LESSONS
PRESERVED FROM THE FIRES OF TIME

DAN L. LAIZURE, DMD, FAGD

Copyright © 2018 by Dan Laizure.

All rights reserved. No part of this book may be used or reproduced in any manner whatsoever without prior written consent of the author, except as provided by the United States of America copyright law.

Published by Advantage, Charleston, South Carolina.
Member of Advantage Media Group.

ADVANTAGE is a registered trademark, and the Advantage colophon is a trademark of Advantage Media Group, Inc.

Printed in the United States of America.

10 9 8 7 6 5 4 3 2 1

ISBN: 978-1-64225-061-9
LCCN: 2018955225

Cover and layout design by Melanie Cloth.

This publication is designed to provide accurate and authoritative information in regard to the subject matter covered. It is sold with the understanding that the publisher is not engaged in rendering legal, accounting, or other professional services. If legal advice or other expert assistance is required, the services of a competent professional person should be sought.

Advantage Media Group is proud to be a part of the Tree Neutral® program. Tree Neutral offsets the number of trees consumed in the production and printing of this book by taking proactive steps such as planting trees in direct proportion to the number of trees used to print books. To learn more about Tree Neutral, please visit **www.treeneutral.com**.

Advantage Media Group is a publisher of business, self-improvement, and professional development books and online learning. We help entrepreneurs, business leaders, and professionals share their Stories, Passion, and Knowledge to help others Learn & Grow. Do you have a manuscript or book idea that you would like us to consider for publishing? Please visit **advantagefamily.com** or call **1.866.775.1696**.

To the most important person in the world to me, my wife Donna, who has been able to get me as close to a state of patience, peace and introspection through her own patience as anyone possibly could. She has allowed me the room to rant and roam the desert that is my mind and provided a safe place to return to be nourished and healed. In short, she puts up with my crap but doesn't rub my face in it. I love her.

Table of Contents

Foreword

I first met Dr. Dan Laizure about twenty-five years ago, when he walked into my small conference room to take a postgraduate class regarding dental treatment. He was a quiet presence in many of my classes over those twenty-five years, however, very early on during one of my classes, he specifically asked if I would mentor him. No one had ever asked me that before, so I was both honored and a little unsure about how we would proceed. Over the years, I have been proud to be his mentor. In fact, *Saving My Library* had a much more significant impact on my life than I could have ever imagined.

Ten years ago, Dan came very close to losing his life, which profoundly changed him. Afterwards, the real and significant difference in him was evident even during a simple conversation.

It is often said that life experience is not the ideal teacher because you get the test before you learn the lesson. However, experience can be the best teacher when it is provided through someone else's experiences. Dan offers that opportunity in his book: to learn how to make positive changes in your life without waiting for the catalyst of a catastrophic event.

Specifically, I love his concept of not being a sea anemone; instead of lying in wait for life's events, opt to be proactive—gain knowledge by design, rather than passively absorbing it. He tells you how to "defend your dreams, your ambitions, and your values."

This is the gift that Dan has provided in *Saving My Library*. He gathers his life experiences to create life lessons for the rest of us. This book also transformed our relationship because he is now my mentor!

Thank you, Dan.

—Dr. John Kois

Acknowledgements

We have all been taught about the "life cycle" in our basic biology classes, which has been popularized as the "circle of life" and I must acknowledge it. At the same time I would like to point out that our individual "circle" is only a single link in an extended chain of life that reaches, I suppose, from the Big Bang to an unknowable future. Even extinction, by our puny definition, cannot eliminate the stardust from which we came and to which we will ultimately return. In the face of Newtonian Physics, only the organization of those elements can be lost or destroyed.

Therefore, as I stand at the center of this nearly infinite chain, I can clearly see only those who most intimately touched my link or those my link may have touched as the chain progresses. Perhaps all I can really see with any clarity is as far back as my grandparents and, at this point, as far forward as my grandchildren. Each of them has individually and collectively influenced and inspired the effort to create this book.

Further, our link is forged from the elements of character we are exposed to and that we choose to incorporate in the alloy of our personal metal. Some of those elements add strength, some add malleability, some bring in flexibility and some make it brittle. At the same time, we are exposed to impurities and contaminates of character that must be smelted from our metal or they may actually weaken our alloy. Each element is carried to us in the personal character of others and it is left to us as to which we will put in the smelting pot of our character.

Since this book is actually about character, perhaps a character, I must acknowledge those who influenced me the most in its creation.

First, my family as I know or knew them in life.

My maternal grandparents, Eugene F. Leitz and Rosa Irene Schubert Leitz, for teaching me the value of hard, physical labor.

My paternal grandparents for giving me my dad. I never knew them except through oral history.

My parents: Mom for teaching me the depths of love, devotion and compassion. No sweeter person ever lived in this world. Dad for giving me, to the degree he could pass on to a stubborn son, tenacity, courage and strength in the face of overwhelming odds.

While these folks are all now deceased, they provided the "base metal" of my single link in the chain of life.

Next, I would like to acknowledge my children and grandchildren for whom this book is specifically written. They are a gift to me from my first wife who, despite our ultimate differences, bore these children whom I love and learn from through their lives and shared experiences and who have continued the chain of life with and through their children.

While the book is dedicated to my wife, Donna, I feel a need to acknowledge her massive, positive influence in the creation of the work also. Dedication is not nearly the acknowledgement she deserves and this is merely another attempt to focus appreciation on the right place.

Also, I want to acknowledge some of the mentors who have had the greatest influence on the creation of this work.

The title and concept of the book is actually attributable to Dr. Ron Wilkins. His conversations and insights are appreciated more than he realizes.

Dr. John Kois, the greatest influence in my clinical practice of dentistry. There is no greater teacher in dentistry than this man.

Walter Hailey (deceased), my mentor, friend and second father. He lives on my shoulder and whispers in my ear daily. I hope my life honors him.

Dr. William Blatchford who, when I was so discouraged and frustrated I wanted to quit dentistry, saved me from that worst of mistakes and started a cascade of mentorship and learning.

All of the coaches, teachers, mentors and friends who have enriched my life and contributed to the essence of this book.

Finally, I must acknowledge and thank the editors and staff of Advantage|ForbesBooks who have likely spent more collective hours getting me through this process than I have drafting, writing and rewriting the entire book.

Thank you all.

My Life-Altering Moment

A master in the art of living draws no sharp distinction between his work and his play; his labor and his leisure; his mind and his body; his education and his recreation. He hardly knows which is which. He simply pursues his vision of excellence through whatever he is doing, and leaves others to determine whether he is working or playing. To himself, he always appears to be doing both.

François-René de Chateaubriand

L ife was good—it usually is, until it isn't. That's where this story begins.

It was 2008. I had created and was running a single dental practice that was generating over $2 million per year in services for our patients and I had my own teaching facility, where I taught continuing dental education to other practicing dentists. The state board of dentistry was pretty impressed with my credentials—enough to give my dental students permission to treat patients under my supervision even when they didn't hold a license in our state. The only thing the board required was that dentists be licensed in their state of residence and bring their patients with them who were also from that state, too. It was a great teaching and learning opportunity.

The facility was gaining positive acclaim and the business of teaching was blossoming when, suddenly, things started going south with my health.

Some days, I'd be going about my daily routine and then lose consciousness, only to regain it a few hours or a day later in the ER or ICU. It was kind of like dying and rising from the dead over and over again. It gave me a new appreciation for Lazarus.

The next fifteen months of my life were spent with physicians specializing in various fields of practice, all focused on one objective: trying to figure out what was wrong with me.

During those fifteen months, doctors proposed diagnoses of everything from brain tumors and neurological issues to varying cardiac and vascular syndromes.

Following a particularly severe "attack" and a more extended stay in the ICU, my primary physician suggested we start over with the diagnostic process. So we did. That is when the correct diagnosis was finally made: one of my heart valves (the aortic) was failing, and it needed to be replaced, *stat*.

The postsurgical recovery was relatively uneventful, even anticlimactic and routine, while the days and weeks of fear and frustration preceding the surgery were enlightening because they forced me to face my own mortality, vulnerability, and weakness.

The experiences pried open my eyes to the reality of life, prompting me to acknowledge that it's made up of much more than just routine tasks—in my case, of drilling, filling, and billing.

My heart valve surgery was a success. I was fine. I knew I would heal, and inside, I was different: wiser, more intuitive, more attuned to my surroundings and to life in general.

I found purpose in each new day. I was much more aware of the importance of each moment beyond the mundane. I began to live with intention and purpose and to realize the impact I had on those around me. I realized that my day-to-day purpose extended much further than just being a country "ivory carpenter," plugging up holes and doling out warnings about gum disease, as important as my profession is to the health and well-being of my patients—brush, brush, floss, floss.

After my recovery, I gave a speech at the Kois Center Symposium to several hundred of the most reputable dentists in the world. The speech was titled "The Doctor as Patient." I was floored by the opportunity and very nervous.

Generally, these symposium talks are expected to be clinical in nature, but I was there to share my insights as a patient and a professional. I had my presentation ready. I knew exactly what I was going to say. I had rehearsed for hours and I was terrified but planned on sticking to the script.

As I stumbled onstage in front of all these people, a spigot burst inside me, and before I knew it, I was there, in front of hundreds of the world's best dental professionals, spewing the feelings, emotions, and life lessons I'd gleaned, from the diagnoses of my heart condition to recovery from my surgery.

Once that spigot was open, attempting to turn it off was like trying to plug a burst fire hydrant with a cotton ball. It just wasn't happening.

I was very apprehensive about the personal nature of this talk as opposed to the clinical one I thought I was expected to give in this venue. I probably sweated through my suit just a little. I can't remember now. What I do remember is my speech coming to a close. I remember my palms slick with sweat as I prepared to leave the stage. I remember being stopped in my tracks by the sudden eruption of applause and standing ovation from this august crowd. I recall the admiration (or sympathy?) in my audience's eyes.

I was both overwhelmed and overjoyed.

As I left the symposium, many people stopped to thank me for my speech and to pepper me with questions about the personal experiences I'd shared. Post-talk, I received several more emails with an onslaught of even more questions, something I'd never anticipated or expected.

That's when I sensed a hunger, when I gained an insight into to what people really wanted, and, in some cases, needed to know. They wanted to hear about life. They wanted to transcend the professional to grasp the personal. They wanted an insight into life. They wanted to learn its lessons. That's why I'm writing this book: to offer my perspective on those lessons.

Life is riddled with teachings, and while I don't claim to be any expert on this topic, I can, through my own experiences and those of others, tell you the ones I think are the most important of all.

That's not the only reason I'm writing this book. To be quite honest, this is my way of documenting my own experiences for myself and for my descendants. I'm not only recording the lessons I've learned but also the mistakes I've made.

I was once told by a good friend that when a dentist dies, it's like burning down a library because of the loss of experience and knowledge. I think that analogy can be extended to say that when all people die, their library is "burned down," which means their lifetime experiences are forever lost, unless they're documented. So many times have I wished that my grandparents, and my parents and aunts and uncles, who were part of "the greatest generation," had left a record of their lives for me and my progeny to read. Their lives might have appeared as mundane and inconsequential to them as mine does to me, but in the evening, by a fire, each of them would reminisce and I would be enthralled. Their struggles, failures, conquests, and in some cases, survival are all a part of my personal heritage and contribute a few words to the history of humanity.

I don't want my "library" to become a pile of ash once I'm gone. I've learned too many valuable lessons that could help many others. That's why I'm writing this book, and if, in the process of this documentation, I end up helping you—even just one person—learn from my experiences, it will be more than worth the effort.

If you're young, you have a special advantage. My advice to you is this: absorb these lessons today, not tomorrow or a year from now. It's easier to make changes when you're younger. It seems to me that as people age, they develop an inertia of bias—they become set in their ways—and it is harder for them to change, despite motivation applied from any but the most severe sources, as in my case. Time passes quickly. As it does, you'll have fewer opportunities to affect your life and the lives of those around you.

Youth offers another advantage. The sooner you start learning and implementing, the longer you have to grow and become the best version of yourself you can possibly be.

Another example that clarifies why you should start young is this: Think of compounded interest and the effect it has over time. The longer your money remains deposited in the account, the more interest it gains, and the more it earns interest on previously accumulated interest Thus even small amounts deposited early can grow to fortunes because the compounding creates exponentially greater returns over time.

The same applies to knowledge and change. Small, positive changes early in life can yield compounded rewards over time. The longer you have to practice those changes, the more you'll become proficient at them, and the more profound the impacts on your life will be.

By the same token, investing later in life is still rewarding, even if that investment doesn't have as much time to compound and grow. So if you're older, don't be discouraged by my compounding analogy and take it to mean that it's too late or not worth your while to act because your rewards won't be as profound as someone who's younger. Instead, think of this book as the sign you've been waiting for to course-correct and make your life even better.

A mentor once told me, "Experience is the worst teacher; it gives the test before it gives the lesson."

On the other hand, my dad had a different philosophy. I loved my dad. I mention him quite a lot in this book because he left a huge imprint on my life and in my heart. I remember he once told me, "Experience is the best teacher, but it doesn't have to be *your* experience that teaches you."

In fact, people who are wise will learn from other's experiences as well as through their own.

If you're familiar with psychology, you might recall Abraham Maslow's pyramidal hierarchy of needs. It theorizes that once we've met the more basic requirements of life, we reach a point of self-actualization. That's where I am: at a point of self-reflection.

It's kind of like driving down a narrow single-lane road into the vast open, looking back in the rearview mirror, and remembering every curve, speed bump, and mile marker. I remember it all, perhaps some parts more vividly and clearly than others.

Our hindsight—our experiences—usually provides us with twenty-twenty vision. They seldom steer us wrong. The problem is we're so fixated on developing our own twenty-twenty foresight, we forget the person next to us might already have had a clarifying experience that could help us—and be willing to share it.

Learn from my hindsight. See life through the clarity of my vision. I'm handing you the lenses. You have the unique opportunity to learn from my experiences, to take what I'm about to share and create a stronger, better, more empowered you.

I hope you chose this book because you're open to receiving advice, or at least considering it, and not because you know me personally and thought you'd be nice and buy it. In any case, you have a choice. You can go through life trying to learn your own lessons and in the end, risk the probability of sorrows and regrets, thinking of what would have happened if you would have, should have, could have done this or that differently. No one wants to live that way. Or you can wisely avoid the craters in the road, walk over the patches, dodge the low-hanging branches, and come out fairly unscathed with fewer regrets.

There's a distinct difference between sorrow and regrets. Sorrow is always a part of our lives, but it's out of our control. You can feel sorrow over someone's passing. You can feel sorrow at someone's fate. You can feel sorrow at your own misfortune. In the end, you must accept or maybe, embrace sorrow.

Regret, on the other hand, is often the result of an action *you* could have controlled but didn't. It's quite preventable. So if you have the opportunity to avoid regrets, take it. I'm handing that opportunity to you on the silver platter of my dental tray in the form of life lessons.

Heed these lessons and apply them to your life. I bet you'll feel happier, more content, and at peace with yourself in the end.

Wishing you every success,
Dr. Dan Laizure

CHAPTER 1

Have Self-Esteem—and Promote It in Others

A s a kid, I was big and fat, and because I was big for my age, I fit right in with my older friends in the neighborhood. One day, when I was only about five, I was hanging out with the big boys and acting my age while they were acting theirs, and I appeared to a neighbor to be "slow." I suppose, because of my weight, I also had a few characteristics associated with down's syndrome, so when I overheard that gentleman say to my mother, "I didn't know Danny was retarded." I took it to heart.

I didn't know I was retarded. The comment caught my five-year-old brain off-guard and made me freeze in my tracks. What was retarded? Was I retarded? When I really thought about it, I realized it might not be far from the truth. I'd never been called that before, but my naïve mind believed it to be true. There was proof too. I was slower to learn than were the rest of the kids my age, so I already felt different, less intelligent. Much later, I'd learn I was dyslexic.

At the time, I didn't realize that this neighbor had made that comment because he assumed I was the same age as the rest of the boys but didn't act like them. Because a grownup said it though, I believed it. I was dumb and slow. It was done. The seed had been planted. Over the years, it would grow into an ugly, stalky, stubborn, thick weed of self-doubt. Those words would reverberate through my mind throughout childhood and into early adulthood, niggling my brain at every opportunity. They would plague me and reinforce negative beliefs within me, making me question my abilities and worth.

It didn't help matters any when, in the third grade, I was pulled out of my regular classroom away from the rest of my classmates to be placed in "remedial reading." At that time, few people had heard of dyslexia or knew about learning disabilities in general, so my dyslexia went unaddressed. Peers assumed I was either dumb or lazy. Add to that the nickname assigned to me by my classmates— "Ten," short for "Ten Tons" —and you can understand why my confidence, by the time I was a young boy in elementary school, was shot.

"Big, fat, dumb, big, fat, dumb" —those words echoed in my head. They're what I heard anytime I looked in the mirror, every time I imagined myself accomplishing anything in life, anytime I tried to identify who I was as I sprung into adolescence.

Overcoming that perception of myself—big, fat, dumb—has been one of the greatest challenges of my life, even when I grew two inches, lost eighty pounds, and looked in the mirror to see my pants fall off.

Even when I won the district wrestling championship for three years out of four in high school and was named as an all-league tackle in football; even after I graduated with honors from college; even when after only three years of college versus the typical four, I was accepted into dental school, where I graduated number two with honors—the mirror reflected big, fat, dumb. I never completely surmounted these doubts.

My deflated self-confidence and belief that I was useless would haunt me for a long time to come. That's the self-image whose shadows I would cower under for the better half of my life.

Later, I'll share with you how I progressed into a more confident man and, eventually, a dentist. The point I want to make now is that today, I realize how different life might have been if I'd believed in myself earlier, if I'd had greater self-esteem, and if I hadn't doubted my true worth and my abilities.

So the first lesson I want to teach you is about the importance of self-esteem, because whoever you are, whatever you do, self-doubt and failing self-confidence are inevitable enemies. We must learn to slay them. In adulthood, the most common example of a lack of self-esteem is imposter syndrome.

IMPOSTER SYNDROME

Whether we're still early in our career, industry experts in our field, or even edging close to retirement, the best of the best of us often doubt our talents and skills.

You fear waltzing into the office one day to see blue lights flashing, police at the ready with handcuffs, and someone shouting into a loudspeaker pronouncing you the imposter and fraud your mind constantly screams you are. Are you really an expert? Do you really know how to do your job well? Are you even worthy of your title or business? Questions like these are extremely common when you're suffering from imposter syndrome.

Unfortunately, this phenomenon is anything but uncommon. Feelings of self-doubt and fear of being recognized for the fake or subpar talent you believe yourself to be are completely normal. You're not suffering alone in these fears, and they can be overcome.

I felt like an imposter early on in life, right around the time I was asked to choose a career path in college.

At the time, young men my age were drafted into the military, and to be honest, I didn't want to have to fight in Vietnam, so I enlisted in the Oregon National Guard instead and was chosen to train in computer repair. This meant a one-year hiatus from college as I went through military training. This didn't guarantee I wouldn't go to Vietnam; it only reduced the likelihood. At the time, it seemed honorable. When the year was up, I returned to campus and found out my councilor had changed. I was advised to speak with my new one before resuming classes, just to make sure I was tracking on target with my courses. My new counselor, Dr. Klein, was a long-haired, radical hippy, whom I didn't think much of at first sight, yet this man ended up changing my life.

He sat across from me, examining me through shaggy locks of hair. "So, what's your plan?" he asked.

With all the confidence and arrogance of youth, I replied, "I'm finishing out this year at Portland State, and then transferring to Oregon State University to pursue a degree in wildlife or marine biology."

Dr. Klein nodded, observing me thoughtfully before he spoke. I restrained from fidgeting under his gaze. "I see by the ring on your finger that you're married. Do you plan on having a family?"

"Of course," I replied, thinking how absurd it was that he'd ask such a silly question.

Unperturbed, he continued. "How do you plan on supporting them?"

"After my degree, I'll find a job with the state or federal government," I said, matter-of-factly.

"Very good," he said. "Now, do me a favor. Look out that window. See all those hippies?"

I tried not to appear surprised at his candor, considering he himself was a bona fide image of a hippy as I'd ever seen. Carefully, I pasted an impassive look on my face and peered out the window, where, sure enough, a crowd of hippies greeted my vision.

Dr. Klein continued, "Nearly every one of those people wants to do what you just described. Many are even willing to work for far less than you and don't have aspirations of marriage or family. Are you willing to compete for a low-paying government job with that large group of people?"

He had me there, but I didn't know what to say. "What choice do I have?"

He flicked through my file, pursing his lips, and then looked up at me through the shaggy curtain of his hair. "You have very good grades, Dan. Have you ever considered the health professions?"

"You mean like a doctor?" I asked, wondering if he'd officially gone off his rocker.

"Well, yes, that's one profession to consider."

"Yeah, sure," I replied. "I actually did think about that, right after I got done thinking about being a cowboy and fireman."

Dr. Klein didn't laugh. He just continued to fasten that same steady gaze on me that penetrated the wall of hair over his eyes and, apparently, my brain.

I gave a resigned sigh. "Medical school is for smart people, Dr. Klein."

"How do you determine who's smart?"

"They have really good grades, well above average."

"Like yours?" he said.

I faltered.

"Son, you're on the honor roll, you're taking some of the most strenuous, albeit lower-division classes, in the school, and you're carrying more than twenty credit hours. Come to grips with the fact that *you are* one of those smart people. Get off your ass and pursue whatever you want—biology, medicine, or whatever else."

I'll never forget Dr. Klein, his hair or, more significantly, the way he opened my eyes to the possibilities that day. That experience was the point of liberation and understanding for me. That was when all the ghosts of the past and the killers of self-esteem began to drop dead like flies after fall's first frost. That meeting, for me, was the start of recognition and realization of self-value and self-worth. It was as if a light had been turned on in my soul.

That light was amazing, but it wasn't always bright. Every now and again, it would grow dim, such as when I was going through dental school. I felt a phony, as if I were trying to be something I couldn't. Eventually, I was able to overcome imposter syndrome, which I'll elaborate on a bit later.

If similar feelings of doubt sprout up in your mind, it helps to find that light inside you. It may be something, or more likely someone, that helps you see your potential. Having a mentor, and, eventually, more than one mentor, is of primary importance as you reflect on your achievements, successes, accolades, and recognition. Left to our own devices, we tend to discount the value of our achieve-ments, but having the support and direction of a mentor helps us see that we do have potential and clarifies what it takes for us to make a success of our self. Mentors help us cling to that light so we can start building a sturdy wall of self-esteem.

HOW TO BUILD OR REBUILD SELF-ESTEEM

Obviously, imposter syndrome isn't the only culprit behind self-esteem issues. Maybe you feel you're not attractive enough for your spouse, or that you're not as great at parenting as your sibling or best friend. Maybe around your coworkers you feel you're about as smart as a grilled cheese sandwich. Insecurity is normal, but it's not okay to be haunted by these thoughts to the point where you start restraining yourself from your true potential.

Doubt is like a fire that ignites with the most infinitesimal amount of fuel. One small drop of the wrong thought can make the mind a devil's workshop of self-destruction.

Before you start building confidence, you have to understand what's causing your self-esteem to suffer. What makes it go spiraling downward out of control? What's the root cause of your doubts and insecurities? Maybe you're able to answer these questions right off the bat, or maybe you find yourself racking your brain, trying to put your finger on what makes those feelings bubble up. If you're having trouble, pay attention the next time these thoughts come to mind and jot down what triggered them.

For me, the root of my self-doubts stemmed from the things I overheard and experienced in my childhood, from being dyslexic to being big and being expected, as a result, to behave older than my age just because I looked it.

I believe what we overhear about ourselves at any age has a deeper impact than what's said, face-to-face, to us. Perhaps, as humans, we tend to shy away from being blatant, honest, and direct with people, face-to-face, to avoid hurting their feelings or being confrontational. However, when we think they're not listening, we feel more at liberty to voice our true feelings and thoughts about them. With that knowledge of our own behavior, we tend to put greater emphasis on what we've overheard people say about us.

Because I overheard the comments I did, my self-esteem began to falter at a young age, only to worsen over time. I carried doubt in my heart for a great part of my life. Even when others saw me as a young, successful man, in the mirror, I saw big, fat, dumb.

Those doubts came barreling forth anytime I set out to make a decision, complete a challenging task, or achieve an objective. "Big, fat, dumb" was my mantra, a solid brick wall standing before me and everything I wanted to accomplish in life. However, now that I knew what had set me off, I could move forward in repairing my self-esteem.

Find out what causes you to doubt yourself and erode your self-confidence. Once you're done figuring that out, it's time to take action and start building, or rebuilding, your self-esteem.

STEP ONE

The best, most surefire way to build your self-esteem is by feeling good about where you are, who you are, or where you're headed. That's why setting a goal and having aspirations in life is an absolute must. What do you want to achieve in life?

For instance, I started off as a biology major. I had direction—sort of. I kind of knew what I was aiming for. In truth, I had little idea of what a marine biologist or a wildlife biologist really did. I would have been at a loss to come up with a job description. It was just a job title that related to a university course description I'd read, and it sounded fun.

Evidently, I had no clue about what I was getting into.

At least I had direction, a goal: I wanted to be a wildlife biologist. As I set that goal into action, I had something to focus my energy and thoughts on instead of wallowing in doubt at every moment.

That's what you have to do: find a direction or a goal. As you take incremental steps—no matter how small—toward it, you'll feel your confidence levels start to buoy.

Although goal-setting is crucial, what's even more important is recognizing when it's time to reset goals. That means once you've achieved your goals, you should set new ones; once a goal no longer appears to be a good fit with your end objective, you have to modify it.

For example, if you achieve a goal—however big or small it may be—and you don't revisit or reset your list of goals, you'll eventually start to drift because you'll grow complacent or you'll feel as if you've already achieved everything you wanted.

For me, not having the next goal in sight is the worst state of life—and everyone around me knows it.

It's not in my nature to stop and party at every milestone. I acknowledge it and maybe cheer a little bit, buy someone a beer or something, but then I move on. If something great happens at the office, I say, "Good job everybody. We're doing great. This is fantastic. I'm so proud of you." I do try to acknowledge others' efforts and show appreciation for what they have contributed, but inside, I'm thinking: *let's work on this.*

One time after we'd achieved some major goals, I gave the team that exact spiel, ending with our next goal to work toward. At that moment, my hygienist looked at me and said, "Aren't you ever satisfied?" My reply to that was, "I'm still breathing. Why would I be satisfied?"

As long as you're alive and kicking, you should be reaching for your next goal, your next objective. The moment you become complacent, you die, because complacency is a killer of potential. Be intentional about what you do, and you'll see the results.

STEP TWO

Once you have a goal, it's time to create an action plan—or a map. Planning is important because a goal without a plan is just a wish. As they say, "If wishes were horses, beggars would ride." Don't be a wisher. Be a doer.

While you're out there creating a map, make sure you're creating the right map. For example, if you're in Hawaii, having a layout of Oregon isn't going to help get you anywhere unless you have some serious water-wings.

If you want to become a chef, putting together a map that's going to help you become a trucker is a waste of time. Make sure your map, or action plan, is well researched and will guide you, at least generally, where you want to go.

Your first ambitions may need to be refined or filtered to become true goals. Mine did. I sometimes think of this process as climbing up a tree. Initially, all you have to do is shimmy up the trunk, but as you climb higher, you have to choose which individual branches you want to tackle, so you have to refine your goals.

Problems arise when people want to change their goal or direction. A change in moving from one branch in the tree to another may be a sequential progression, not causing a problem if the new branch lies in the planned general direction. Merely keep climbing, moving upward along branches that can lead to greater refinements.

On the other hand, the view from a "higher" position (newly acquired experience, knowledge, and/or understanding) may prompt you to move to other branches in the same tree (or discipline), that may require a leap, or a Tarzan-like swing if the gap between the new goal and your current track is too wide. Often, backtracking is the safest way to accomplish a major change—even in the same discipline—and it almost always is if you're choosing a new disciplinary "tree."

If, after conscientious consideration, you do decide to make a major goal change, and you are willing to pay the price in terms of your emotional and financial health, and time, then go for it, especially if your core values are better served by taking the new direction.

Nonetheless, for heaven's sake, stop and think and consider and examine the price and payoff of your decision. Don't act like a monkey swinging back and forth, thinking you are a Tarzan with a direction, when all you are doing is making noise and drawing attention to yourself.

Once you have the right map in place, orient it correctly to your "true north," your core values and principles.

Remember, your core values should be values *you* hold dear and personal. These are values that mean something to *you*. They're not values you're taught by the five Ps in your life: parents, peers, preachers, professors and (in my case) patients. They're not what a political party or your therapist wants you to believe or value.

A relatively quick, though brutal, way to discover your core values is to imagine yourself at your own funeral. What do you want said about you at that point? Usually the things you want to hear about yourself are the attributes and actions that reflect your core beliefs and values.

It's then that you can sit down with confidence and say, "This is who I am. This is what's important to me," even if that's completely at variance with what everyone around you believes to be important.

Once you know your core values, it's time to locate and connect the dots between the two most important points on your map: where you are and where you want to be.

Wise travelers will take it a step further and examine the terrain and everything between where they are and where they want to go. They'll figure out the obstacles and create a pathway to avoid or overcome those obstacles, making sure to never do anything that deviates from their true north.

We'll talk more about true north in later chapters, too, because they're the core of life.

STEP THREE

You are what you think. So the third step is to make sure you're being optimistic and self-affirming. Affirmations are positive thoughts and statements chosen carefully to restructure and strengthen your mind's belief in positive outcomes. Once you have the power of a positive mind on your side, it can lead you to great doorways of opportunity and help you progress toward your goals.

A couple of personal affirmations I have used for more than twenty years were taught to me by my mentor Walter Hailey: "I am healthy, wealthy and happy and I get what I want because I deserve it," and "I always do what I ought to do, when I ought to do it, whether I want to or not, with no debate." These two simple statements repeated at least once a day in the morning have served me very well in overcoming many of the inner goblins of doubt that would have continued to hamper my personal achievement.

Affirmations should be positive, in the first-person possessive, and descriptive of the attributes you desire. Don't worry about whether you actually have the attributes you desire. The whole idea is to convince your mind that you are the person you describe. Your mind has no filter and will accept whatever you tell it, good or bad.

Other examples of self-affirmation could be expressions as simple as, "Today I am full of wisdom and strength," and "My marriage is stronger and better today than it was yesterday" as long as the words are meaningful to you. The deeper the personal meaning and the more specifically the affirmation addresses an issue, the more effective it will be. Positive thoughts are known to turn into positive actions, so it's important to infuse positivity in your mind to see it come to fruition in your life.[1]

STEP FOUR

Once you restructure your mind to eradicate negative thinking, replacing it with encouraging, powerful affirmations, it's time to start your journey. You can do that alone, but it's best if you have a

---

1   Carmen Harra, "35 Affirmations That Will Change Your Life," Huffpost, July 15, 2017, https://www.huffingtonpost.com/dr-carmen-harra/affirmations_b_3527028.html

guide, or a mentor, to lead the way. This person should be someone who is experienced, has already traveled this same journey, and can hold your hand, decipher the map, and get you going in the right direction.

I was fortunate enough to find my guide about ten years into my dental career, after which, my imposter syndrome began fading like morning fog on a summer day.

My mentor, a fellow named Walter Hailey, was probably all of about five-feet-four-inches tall. A squat little grandpa-like guy who owned a dental marketing company, he taught me about so much more than just marketing.

I took my staff to hear him speak one day. He delivered an inspiring speech and left us with tasks to complete. We returned to him a few months later. This time I came prepared with a business plan and gave everyone on my staff a copy of it.

"Look," I told them, "when we're at Walter's course, write your ideas in the margins of this plan. Don't worry about writing down what he and the other speakers say; write down what they stimulate you to think about, what ideas you get from listening to them." So that's what we all did, though I was doing it maybe a little less covertly than they were.

Next thing you know, Walter's standing over me, and there I am, writing something in the margin.

"Well, what have you got there?" he asked.

I felt my face grow warm. "Just something I've worked on," I replied.

"Can I see?"

I handed over the whole stack of the accordion-type paper that the old dot matrix printers used back then. He peered at me over his half glasses, took the stack of conjoined papers, and kept flipping through the pages, pausing to look at each page and glance at me before looking at another page and darting me another look.

Oh, crap, I thought, *I've really pissed him off.*

"Can I share this with the rest of the group?" he asked.

I hesitated, but unable to see a way out, I nodded.

He went up to the lectern in front of this class of about a hundred, held up the first page and let the rest of the tractor feed swoosh down to the floor in a gigantic scroll.

"Dan here," he announced to the class, keeping his gaze locked on me, "has prepared the best darned business plan for dentistry I've ever seen. I want all of you dentists to see this—and none of you can have it."

I'm sure my mouth was probably on the floor.

"Dan," he continued, from his position center-stage, "Will you have breakfast with me in the morning?"

I was flabbergasted. What was I going to say? "No, go screw yourself?" So after I fumbled to find my voice, I managed a quick nod and a confident affirmation.

"Great. See you at four-thirty," he said. The man was a bag of surprises. Breakfast at 4:30 a.m. Who'd ever imagine?

Aside from an invitation to breakfast at a time of night when most sleepwalkers are enjoying their craft, I gained something I really needed at that point in my profession: validation.

Not only did Walter's comment validate me to myself; it validated me to my staff.

The old saying, "You're never a prophet in your own land," is absolutely true. That day, Walter made me a prophet to my staff. I was catapulted from dumb, old-country, you're-not-smart-enough-to-do-dentistry-in-the-big-city-so-you-moved-to-bodunk-Walla-

Walla to someone who was worthy of praise from the acclaimed Walter Hailey.

Because I'd earned praise from an authoritative figure who had many accomplishments to his name, my staff treated me differently—or perhaps I just acted differently. Who knows? In reality, I think it's mostly the former. Employees who used to drag their feet at my requests were now snapping to attention, eager and pleased to do things I suggested. It was a breath of fresh air.

Validation is integral to developing yourself and gaining self-esteem. In fact, we all strive for validation in our lives, validation of who we are, along with our successes. In fact, this book, in many ways, serves as a validation of my accomplishments.

Until Walter, I didn't fully have the self-esteem I needed. Because he himself was successful, his validation of me gave me the mantle of credibility I needed. That's what's so great about mentors. They build you into who you want to be but also give you the stamp of approval you need to let you know you've passed, you've made it.

WHY BUILD SELF-ESTEEM?

It might have crossed your mind that despite my self-esteem issues, I was able to manage a pretty decent life for myself and my family through my career as a dentist. So why even bother focusing on self-esteem?

The truth is I think I could have achieved a lot more if I hadn't doubted myself. Self-esteem, confidence, trust in yourself—all of it—can help you achieve your goals and see successes so much sooner and more easily. That's not to say you can't achieve successes when you don't have those things—I'm living proof that it's possible—but attaining goals when you're confident is like walking around without a load on your shoulders. You're able to run, sprint, leap, and scale higher mountains when there's no burden weighing you down. On the other hand, lack of self-esteem is like trying to go rock climbing carrying a small boulder on your back; it's still doable but so much more difficult and time consuming, not to mention emotionally and physically draining.

NATURE VERSUS NURTURE

Many of you readers might stop right here and say, "Yeah, well, Dr. Laizure, everything you've said is dandy. I'm glad you got your self-esteem back. I'm glad all this worked out for you, but you don't know my situation. It's easier for you to build your self-esteem than it is for me. You weren't born with one leg shorter than the other. You don't have my father. You don't have my mother. You don't have my challenges. You haven't walked a mile in my shoes."

That's true. No one is you. No one is going through what you are in exactly the way you are, but I think there's something to consider here that says a lot about how you process that fact.

Either you can take that knowledge and continue to blame nature for your fate and insecurities, or you can nurture yourself into being successful and more self-confident, overcoming the obstacles in your path. Probably, the only thing you'll gain from the first option is bitterness. The second option gives you a greater shot at seeing promising results.

If you're willing to nurture yourself, you'll need to practice maturity, honesty, and even brutal introspection to see what you can do, how you can be different, and how you can expand yourself beyond your self-perceived limitations. Above all, *you* are the one who must make the decision to address the self-esteem issue. As strange as it might sound, no one can do it for you. It must be a completely self-initiated process.

In my dental practice, I have a long-established history of helping people quit using chewing tobacco, which is somewhat euphemistically referred to as "spit tobacco." After helping many people ditch this habit and addiction, I have found one truth to be ever present: individuals must want to quit for themselves. The first question I ask prospective patients is why they are trying to quit. If they tell me it's because their wife/girlfriend wants them to quit, I tell them I cannot help. Until they commit to quitting because they want to, there is no sense in their wasting my, or their, time.

A lot of negative self-talk goes along with low self-esteem, just as it does in quitting the use of tobacco. You have to quit the habit of negative self-talk, but taking that first step, making that decision, is paramount.

Most people stretch themselves to fill the "box" they build in their own minds, but every box has walls. This means we restrict ourselves to our own pre-established limits. Instead of living in a box, live in a bubble. Let the walls around you grow and stretch, and let yourself expand emotionally and intellectually.

You must be willing to invest in yourself. You've heard that before, but I'm going to elaborate and tell you to invest in yourself and invest early on.

On several occasions, I have had patients who needed and asked for what we call a "full mouth reconstruction." The need for this type of extensive, very expensive, treatment usually occurs because of years of inadequate maintenance or just plain old neglect. On two occasions, I have completed these reconstructions and the results were beautiful, and the patients were ecstatic.

The downer occurred a year or so later when, despite extensive instructions and the admonition that regular in-office as well as at-home maintenance was imperative, these patients failed to follow instructions and ended up returning only after the entire reconstruction was failing. On these two occasions, the patients opted to have the dental restoration done despite the hefty cost. Unfortunately, their restoration failed again, for the same reason, and they ended up having to have a full set of dentures. (I suppose a contributing factor might also have been that the costs involved in treatment were funded through a trust fund in one case and a boyfriend in the other case, so neither patient really had any "skin in the game.")

However, my point is that, in any aspect of life, you must commit to ongoing maintenance, even if you end up having to drag yourself up by your boot straps. Self-esteem and self-confidence are never-ending, ever-evolving qualities, and you're the one who is solely in charge of fostering them.

Don't wait too long to fix yourself when you see your confidence plummeting or something else about you going downhill. Invest in yourself early on and continually. Don't let the minor cracks and flaws turn into gaping, irreparable holes. Polish yourself and continue polishing yourself until you can polish no more. Figuratively speaking, brush, brush, and floss, floss.

PROMOTING SELF-ESTEEM IN OTHERS

Life is more than about just developing and shaping yourself. As I mentioned earlier, this world needs mentors. It needs people who can help others to go up and over. So go above promoting self-esteem within just yourself and help others build it too. When you start giving is when you start achieving joy and fulfillment in life. You'll find that doing so will help you feel good and gain the respect of others, which will foster a greater sense of self-respect within you and increase your own self-esteem.

One way to build self-esteem in others is by becoming their validator, as Walter Hailey once was for me. Or you can do it by paying honest compliments or giving encouragement. You could share your skills and knowledge. You could tutor or train. There are many ways to go about it.

Here's the thing about giving: you can't get water out of an empty pitcher. To share something, you first have to possess it yourself, whether that's self-esteem or something else. So before you try to help someone else develop self-esteem, develop it within yourself. Otherwise, your efforts will be void.

Now that you're well on your way to becoming a more self-confident you, we're ready to move on to the next great lesson: never make assumptions.

CHAPTER 2

Don't Make Assumptions

Years ago, I had a patient named Nancy. She's no longer alive, but Nancy was one of my favorites, and I always looked forward to her visits. On one of them, she shared a humorous anecdote about something that happened one night when she was at her cabin in the mountains.

Nancy and some of her friends were playing cards when, suddenly, a strange noise startled them. It was a new moon and pitch black outside when she went to investigate her front yard, and that's when she saw it: a big, black steer. Because her cabin was in the middle of an open range, Nancy wasn't surprised, but she was a little disgruntled since the animal could damage her plants.

I should probably tell you that Nancy was a tiny little thing, maybe five feet tall, tops, which meant she often had to depend on her considerable verbal skills, developed from her experience as an English teacher working at the state penitentiary in Walla Walla, to be taken seriously. She also had a pleasant but feisty character, which meant she wasn't going to tolerate sass from a steer.

The animal was facing away from her, so Nancy walked out of the cabin on tiptoes, brandishing an open palm, determined to resolve the situation. When she came within range, she drew back her hand and was about to smack the animal on its behind. Before she struck the north end of the south bound animal, the steer rose onto its hind legs and looked at her over its shoulder. Nancy was instantly transfixed in shock and amazement. The animal had suddenly morphed from a steer to a bear.

The bear barked a muffled "woof," dropped down on all four legs, and scampered off into the dark woods, leaving Nancy completely befuddled and shaken. She'd almost smacked a bear because she'd played into the assumption that the animal in her yard was a steer rather than the much more dangerous bear. She's lucky that bear didn't attack her, or try to bite off her head. We're not always so fortunate in life, which brings us to our next lesson: don't assume. Things aren't always as they appear. Only when we take time to inspect people and situations closer to glean more information can we arrive at the best decision, or judgment.

Sometimes it's tough not to assume, because that's asking you to do the opposite of what you've been trained to do for so many years. Deduction is a natural tendency in humans and even encouraged in academia, but sometimes we take what we consider to be facts and draw conclusions from them. Often, these conclusions turn out to be assumptions that might at first appear logical or rooted in common sense, but you can probably think of at least a few times when your own assumptions were proved incorrect and cost you something valuable.

In most circumstances, it's never prudent to make assumptions when you're not completely clear about the circumstances. Avoid being overconfident in yourself and strive to draw conclusions from things grounded in solid facts rather than in assumptions. Sometimes an incorrect assumption can cost you a lot—maybe even your life, as it almost did with me.

We live in a valley, and usually, wildlife stays up in the mountains, but on one occasion, a very large cougar ventured down to kill sheep, dogs, and cats. This particular cougar had broken one of its upper canine teeth, which had become abscessed. As any of you who have had a dental abscess know, this condition can be extremely painful. This particular cat was not able to ply his normal trade on healthy mountain wildlife since he did not have the normal, deadly compliment of "tools." He was driven by hunger to attack domestic animals for sustenance, and because he was dangerous to humans and livestock in my valley, I found myself tracking him, using a pack of dogs.

One morning, after a particularly long and uncomfortable hunt, I found him crouching in a tree and shot him with my wife's .357 pistol. It was a solid shot, and it should have proved fatal, but the cat managed its way out of the tree and took off, the dogs hot on his trail. After a few minutes, their barking changed: they started using a kind of bark that let me know they'd somehow lost track of the cougar and its scent. I didn't understand how that was possible. How could he have gotten away after being shot? Although there was no blood visible, I knew he was badly wounded. He shouldn't have been able to escape the dogs.

After reloading, I went down to investigate, and sure enough, I saw the pack milling about in the snow. There was a large maple tree that the cat would ordinarily have scaled, but the dogs weren't paying attention to its trunk. I walked toward the maple, right to where the dogs were milling about, looking for cat tracks. There weren't any.

Just then, I heard a low growl directly above and behind me. It was the cougar. Apparently, he'd run down a little hill and jumped directly onto a limb that was twelve to fifteen feet off the ground, which explained why there was no scent for the dogs to follow.

I was directly underneath the cougar, completely vulnerable and a potential meal, from his perspective. In that brief moment, I realized how gravely I'd misjudged the situation, how completely I'd misread the signs, and how royally I'd screwed up to the point where I might have to pay with my life.

I spun around and brought my pistol to bear, fully expecting the cougar to have already launched himself at me. Luckily, he remained crouched on the limb, and I was able to deliver a final fatal shot without being attacked.

The lesson here is clear: pay attention and don't ever assume. I had misjudged the situation completely by trusting that the entire hunt would progress step-by-step, exactly as I'd been taught, experienced, and read in books. I followed the instructions to a tee, and then waltzed in, assuming that the problem had been resolved as it had been on other occasions. Obviously, it wasn't. I assumed I'd shot the cougar, and even when he escaped, I assumed the dogs wouldn't lose track of a wounded animal, and when I walked under that tree, I assumed I was safe. Assumptions can cost you dearly. Avoid them.

In the end, we're humans, and no matter how much I preach, we all—me included—still end up making assumptions, at some point or another, even if we don't mean to. You see your friend whispering to someone right after you've had a heated argument and you assume they're talking about you. You find a receipt for a late-night dinner in your spouse's blazer and assume your spouse has been cheating you.

We all make assumptions, which brings me to another important point: saying sorry when your assumptions lead you awry.

ASSUMPTIONS AND APOLOGIES

When you make an incorrect assumption, an apology is non-negotiable. Learn to say, "I'm sorry." Offer restitution or make it up to the injured party, somehow. Learning to apologize is humbling, liberating even.

I learned the power of apology from a patient who was always sort of persnickety. One day, she left a message with my receptionist, asking me to return her call so she could discuss an incident that had taken place at our office. I remember thinking, *Oh, crap, now I'm going to have to call her and listen to her go bat crazy on me.* Reluctantly, I picked up the receiver, dialed her number, and cringed when she answered. To my utter shock and surprise, however, she was, perhaps, the sweetest she'd ever been.

In fact, she started off our conversation offering an apology for the incident. She said she realized she'd been unfair in her judgment and wanted to explain that she'd recognized the error of her ways and was sorry.

That takes guts. I can honestly say that after our call, I had a newfound respect for her.

We should all strive to be that person, to be able to say, "Yeah, I screwed up. I made a mistake. Will you forgive me?"

Once we ask for forgiveness, it puts the onus on the other person to do what's right.

So when you make a mistaken assumption, don't be too timid to apologize, which brings me to another point. Even though we say we shouldn't assume, we're sometimes placed in a situation where we're forced to assume, such as when we're developing trust in a relationship.

THE RELATIONSHIP BETWEEN TRUST AND ASSUMPTION

Some of our greatest successes come from working as members of a team, which requires an element of trust. Business partners have to trust each other, spouses have to trust each other, even teachers and students have to practice a certain degree of trust with one another, but when we're collaborating to build that trust, there's a certain point at which we have to *assume* trust. In a partnership, you might assume that you'll each fulfill your obligations or that you won't steal from each other or that you'll guide each other the right way or that you'll fulfill a promise.

When that assumption of trust is violated, it's called betrayal. History is full of it.

Just look at the story of Judas and Jesus. Jesus, prior to being crucified, had known that one of his disciples would betray him. He even went as far as to declare this knowledge at his last supper. Before announcing his suspicions to those present, Jesus humbled himself by washing the feet of everyone there, including Judas, who turned out to be his betrayer, and turned Jesus over to the authorities to have him executed.

Take a peek into your own life and you'll see that trust isn't betrayed just in religion or history books. It's all around us.

For years, my practice had been lagging, and I couldn't fathom why. I was working harder than I ever had, seeing more patients, and doing more work than ever before, but somehow, I was constantly falling short of capital to reinvest into the practice.

Even after infusing over $280,000 from my personal savings into my business, I was forced to lay off staff so I could make payroll. These were great people in both the human and professional sense, so letting them go was a difficult and painful decision. We parted company in tears, and I realized I had to figure out the problem and solve it quickly before my entire practice went belly up.

Several years earlier, I'd hired a man named Davie, an economics professor, to manage my check register and also perform some minor bookkeeping tasks for the practice. Not very easy on the eyes, Davie was aptly dubbed "the troll" by some of the other employees, but I liked him because he seemed to be loyal.

They say good judgment comes from experience, and most of that experience comes from bad judgment. I misjudged this man.

One evening, on a whim, I decided to take a closer look at my check register, not suspecting any fishy business. At about three in the morning, after poring over the numbers, I woke my wife and asked her if we had any credit card accounts in Virginia. She said we didn't. I also noticed several checks written as refunds to a previous employee, who had not had any dental services performed for several years.

Perturbed, I took the information I'd discovered to my CPA and asked him if I had the problem I thought I had. He confirmed my suspicions and the Gordian knot of financial intrigue was finally exposed. I'm a little less patient than Alexander the Great, so I immediately fired Davie, since I couldn't cut off his head due to the social customs of the modern world.

When I told Davie he was dismissed—I didn't tell him I'd discovered his treachery—he immediately blurted out that I owed him $8,000, but that we could work something out. I held my peace through an iron will, although it took everything in me not to whip out my drill and take out his left eye. As it turned out, through my own misplaced trust and loyalty, the maggot had stolen over $1,200,000 dollars over five years, starting from the time I had been diagnosed with a failing heart valve. Davie was found guilty and sentenced to prison in 2014. Although I was marginally satisfied with his being behind bars, I knew it wouldn't help me reclaim my lost efforts, lost time, the phenomenal employees I'd let go, or the money I'd sacrificed in trusting him. Luckily, I do get victims compensation to the tune of $260 a month, which should get me paid off with no interest in roughly 384.6 years. All this was thanks to a misplaced assumption of trust.

How do we overcome this hurdle? How do we assume trust and establish relationships without getting burned? We can start by learning from our fortieth president.

RONALD REAGAN'S PHILOSOPHY ON TRUST

The secret behind any great leader is his ability to delegate, but delegation requires trust. President Ronald Reagan was popularly known for his ability to run his presidency by trusting people to do what was expected of them, but he had a motto to back up his philosophy: trust and verify.

Instead of simply trusting his staff to execute tasks completely, Reagan was often known to sporadically also verify the successful execution of each task to make sure it was completed satisfactorily, in turn reaffirming his faith in that individual.

In the same way, when you're assuming trust to build a partnership or relationship, always verify. For example, don't do what I did and allow people to have blind control over a single aspect of your business without ever validating that trust and verifying their work.

UNDERSTANDING PEOPLE WHEN TRUSTING

I'm starting this section with great trepidation and concern because I'm apprehensive about advising on social mores without losing sight of the moral point I'm trying to convey. People usually aren't whom or what they show you, which makes it difficult to trust or know anyone completely. In fact, there are very few people who are truly transparent. I believe there are usually at least two people in each person: the public persona and the private core manifestation. Sometimes people don't even know themselves until some test of character arises.

What people display to the world is a façade. This is seldom who they really are. Only time and tests can uncover the gold or dross that they carry inside. Conversely, the private core is what people are when nobody is watching, not even the people closest to them such as their spouse, children, parents, and siblings. I have heard this described as character. The presentation displayed publicly is for public consumption but often doesn't jive with the private reality. For example, outwardly, your friend may make her life out to be perfect, both professionally and personally: a rewarding career, a huge house, the perfect husband. Privately, however, only she and her spouse truly know their finances are strained and their relationship is suffering from fractures.

By the same token, you might have a coworker who brown-noses the boss, when, in fact, he hates working for him and the company.

Most of us use a different language in public from the one we use in private, which isn't necessarily a bad thing. It's just more convenient this way. It's easier, more peaceful, and simpler to differentiate your public behavior from your private behavior.

Several years ago, Jim Carey starred in a humorous movie that demonstrated the social shortcomings of being completely frank.

Know this: the further apart a person's two personas are, the less trustworthy that individual maybe.

Sometimes the brutally honest are the loneliest people around. They may be the truest friends and are the least likely to lead you astray from your own moral code if you can stand the brutal truths they dish out like ice cream.

It's important to be aware of people's dual personas before you assume trust. Understand that people are seldom what they appear to be. There's always another side, a different character they play when few are watching. So don't assume trust; let it be built.

Remember there are heroes among us and there are villains among us. You can't always tell who's who. You could be at a bar, sitting with a crowd of people who are genuine heroes, and you'd never know because they often won't tell you. On the other hand, there could be a villain disguised as a hero in your church, but all you see is his pious side. We all have hidden personalities, just as we all have latent fears and undisclosed strengths.

This leads us to another relevant life lesson and the next chapter of this book: don't judge.

CHAPTER 3

Don't Prejudge; Practice Acceptance

A t a very young age, Mom, in her effort to try and educate me while realizing that reading was not my strong point, bought me a recording of some poetry. For some reason or other, I was drawn to that recording, enjoying several of its poems, and one particular poem that's still one of my favorites, Rudyard Kipling's *Gunga Din*. As you may know, it's a poem about a "regimental bhisti," or water carrier, named Gunga Din, who was an Indian with dark skin. The soldier from whose perspective the story is told is prejudiced, but toward the end of the poem, he realizes his shortsightedness:

An' for all 'is dirty ' ide,
'E was white, clear white, inside
When 'E went to tend the wounded under fire!

The whole poem is a reprimand of human prejudice and a call to humanity that ends,

> Tho' I've belted you an' flayed you,
> By the living Gawd that made you,
> You're a better man than I am, Gunga Din!

That's what this chapter's lesson is about: avoiding prejudice.

I witnessed the grotesque effects of facial injuries from war at a young age, even spending several hours in the hospital with my own father, who, as a marine of the 1st Marine Division, had fought and been injured during the Korean conflict. I wasn't naïve about the havoc war could wreak on people and their bodies. In fact, I was hyperaware of it.

My mother used to recount a story about a time when we were traveling across the interstate bridge, a drawbridge, between Portland, Oregon, and Vancouver, Washington. We were on our way to visit my dad at the US Department of Veterans Affairs (VA) hospital where he was in recovery. The bridge was up, and as we waited, I climbed on the front seat of our old 1936 Chevy, looked out the passenger window, and immediately started saying, "That poor woman. Oh, that poor woman."

My mom craned her neck to follow my line of vision to the car next to ours, where an African-American lady was behind the wheel. In my naivety, because I had never seen a black person before, I assumed she'd been burned or injured in a combat catastrophe. I used my own experiences to draw a conclusion, an assumption.

In my case, the assumption turned out to be harmless. I gleaned something from it. Some years later, when my mother retold this story, I learned that while we are different on the outside—we don't all look exactly alike—we're all human and part of the same great family.

We didn't see a lot of racial diversity in Milwaukie, the small town just southeast of Portland where I lived. Heck, it was a major event when one of my wrestling teammates had a black opponent from another school. In our cloistered little environment, virtually everybody was white. My mother, in her wisdom, made sure I understood that all people were created the same, regardless of how they appeared on the surface.

One of her favorite examples was our dogs.

We'd always had dogs in our family, and my mom knew how much I loved them. "Look," she used to say. "Some of these dogs are black, some are brown, others are mixed, but we love them all the same, don't we?" She would always add, "I think God made us all and he loves us all no matter what color our skin is, just like you love your dogs. He wants us all to love and care about each other the same way."

Thanks to her, at a young age, I already understood the importance of loving humans equally, of not prejudging people because of the color of their skin, their religious beliefs, or their nationality. I learned to accept people as diverse beings.

My mother would be pleased to know this lesson has stuck with me throughout my life. It's one I still embrace to this day. I'm a firm believer in human equality and brotherhood, regardless of creed or origin.

My wife and I have spent some time in Africa. In some areas of the continent, there's this blatant antagonism between blacks and whites. I went hunting in the African bush, and I hired a tracker, a black guy, who was working really hard to make sure that I, as a rookie, was safe. He was called a tracker, but he was, basically, a servant, rifling through the forests and foliage barefoot among piercing thorns, risking his own life to make sure there were no snakes endangering mine. During hunting activities, he ventured ahead of me, acting as my human shield. If I wanted water, he'd fetch it for me before I could even ask. Every time I'd turn around, he was right there, my shadow of protection. This man did everything to protect me. At the end of my trip, as a token of my appreciation, I felt ashamed of pulling out a measly $100 to tip him for his efforts. I felt like an absolute piker despite knowing that I was being generous by the standards of the region and industry. That paltry amount, I knew, was unfair compensation for what this man had done for me. However, when the owner of the lodge, a white guy, found out, he went berserk: "That's as much as he earns in a year and you gave him $100? Are you stupid?" he bellowed.

"Well, then, you should pay him better," I retorted. "You're a cheap bastard, and it's not my fault you don't pay him enough."

That incident rattled me, to say the least, because it was so telling of the open animosity between the blacks and whites, which goes both ways. The whites felt that the blacks were of a lower order. The blacks didn't like the whites, and in one case in Zimbabwe, burned to the ground the lodge we had stayed in and "repatriated" the land and holdings of the white owners. Frankly, in the context of this writing, I do not want to make a judgment or comment regarding the actions or morality of either side of the issue other than to note the bad feelings that exist on both sides.

My belief is and always will be that skin color doesn't reveal a person's integrity. Religion doesn't guarantee a person's piety or benevolence. At the end of the day, such differences do nothing to let you read beyond people's obvious physical traits to their character.

Skin color, nationality, origin—all these things are shallow variations. They bear no reflection on who we are at our core.

If we are psychologically healthy, without sociopathic flaws, we all cry, we all love, we all fear, we all dream, we all have empathy and kindness, and we all practice humanity in different ways.

I'll use my professional experiences to demonstrate. I remember collecting extracted teeth (puke!) in dental school and preserving them in antifreeze. With time, I learned to discern diseased teeth from healthy ones, eventually becoming experienced enough to identify different types of teeth coming from the same mouth. Each tooth was different. They were unique, and I might have been able to identify them as belonging to the same mouth, but I could never tell the race, religion, or country of origin of the person to whom the teeth had belonged.

My point is we're all unique—all of us—but we're not unique because of the color of our skin or the origins of our ancestors or the beliefs of our families. That which makes us human remains the same from individual to individual. Self-awareness, reason, intellect and the ability to make choices are much more important and bind us together as a whole species much more tightly than the petty, superficial differences that so many focus on to tear us apart. It's our heart and our soul that determine our internal, maybe even eternal, nature.

Those of you who are religious may have been taught the commandment "Love thy neighbor." You're not taught "Love thy neighbor only if he looks like you." We're taught to celebrate our differences, to respect one another, to help one another—no barriers accepted.

Empathizing, communicating, and keeping company exclusively with those whom you deem to be exactly like you risks developing into bigotry, which limits your understanding, closes your mind, and makes you see life through a narrow lens. Bigotry is a self-imposed limitation that can develop into hostility. Humans are not meant to be exactly the same. To practice bigotry is to short-change yourself, because in setting limits to your understanding of the world, you lose out on what could lead to amazing friendships and experiences.

Don't limit your thinking. Don't limit your perception of others based on what meets the eye or skin-deep knowledge. A wise person will observe, unearth, and analyze others carefully, layer by layer, before drawing a conclusion about their character, credibility, integrity, and so on.

THE POWER OF WORDS AND THE DETRIMENT OF JUDGMENT

There's a poster that reads, "All I need to know, I learned in kindergarten." When it comes to your interactions with people, several of those aphorisms from our childhood prove true even today, and they will forever.

Another aphorism cautions that if you can't say something nice, don't say anything at all. As I explained in chapter 1, one person's words about me had an extremely detrimental effect on much of my life, unbeknownst to the person who had uttered them.

The words we speak and hear, for good or for ill, can affect us permanently, because words can long outlive the moment when they're expressed. As is said from time to time, "You cannot un-ring a bell."

While negative words can cause damage far beyond the emotional horizon, positive words can lend encouragement and support far beyond the emotional horizon. We must choose our words wisely lest we do unintended harm when we could just as easily have done some good.

I have always believed that if you discover you were wrong about something and are forced to eat your words, it's much easier for you to swallow the sweet than the bitter. I'd rather say something generous about someone, find I was wrong, and have to say, "Well, maybe I misjudged. That person is not quite as nice as I thought." That's much better than saying something really nasty about someone only to find out that person is actually amazingly good-natured.

DON'T SELF-POISON WITH PREJUDICE

When you prejudge, you're assuming, as fact, information for which there is no evidence, whether it's about a person or a situation. This means you're pulling from a limited pool of knowledge. You've literally closed yourself off to exploring and learning beyond what you already know, or think you know, based on incomplete information, which, in turn, prevents your mind from growing and expanding. You keep retrieving the same knowledge, over and over again, hindering your growth and limiting your perceptions of the world. You never delve into a situation deeper than the surface.

People who are limited in their thinking are perceived to be limited in their intelligence too. Prejudiced thoughts are harmful enough without expressing such thoughts. My father always used to say, "It is better to keep quiet and be thought a fool than to open your mouth and remove all doubt." So act and think and speak slowly.

If you remember Nancy's encounter with the bear, you'll see that, often, things are not as they initially appear to be, which is why you'd be wise to withhold assumptions and judgments. Give people a chance to build their credibility, to gain your trust, to prove their worth. We are all designed as unique individuals who have something to offer.

Imagine if everyone made decisions in every aspect of life based on what they first saw or perceived. Our understanding of people and the universe would be dramatically limited if there were no patient research or discovery. Even our progression as a species would be limited. We'd dwell in a narrow tunnel, never seeing a glimpse of the light outside.

Everything in life has dimension and character, and all of us have more depth to our character than meets the eye. If you're focused on the outer shell, you'll never enjoy the best part of all: the center, the essence. It's like eating the skin of a fruit and tossing the pulp!

Beyond limiting your own perception, prejudices can also damage your business or professional progress.

Businesses are competitive: whoever snags the most clients reaps the greatest rewards. Realistically speaking, no single business can have the entire market share. Ideally, everyone will get a chunk of the pie. When you limit your business dealings to just a certain race, nationality, creed, and so on, you're only welcoming a sliver of your potential business. It doesn't make economic sense, even if you ignore the moral aspect of your actions.

At the same time, don't be nice to people just for the sake of stealing the market share. Be genuinely and whole-heartedly open-minded, unprejudiced, compassionate, and caring of all people. If you're just welcoming them through your doors as a ploy to make money, your motive will surely be exposed at some point, costing you business, integrity, and self-respect, at the very least.

I live by example. Our office exists to care for people—all people. I believe that because we come from a good place in our hearts, we've been successful as a business, earning rewards and recognition throughout the years. Our team is comprised of talented individuals who've amassed that talent through many different channels. We'll never be able to truly pinpoint all the hands and resources to which we're indebted for creating all the talent that has contributed to our success today. So we have no right to put restrictions on the number of people whom we will repay.

Prejudice can impede our ability to work well with others, which can cause the most damage to our own professional growth.

I once decided I wanted to hire a Hispanic lady so we could better communicate with patients who didn't speak English as well as they did Spanish. I explained this to my office manager, and we duly hired a Hispanic, but she soon resigned, which I didn't think too much about at the time. Later, I described to the office manager the skills and responsibilities I foresaw for a Spanish-speaking employee. The office manager looked at me and said, "You'll never find one of *them* who wants to work that hard."

"One of them? What do you mean?"

"You'll never find a Mexican who'll work that hard."

That comment pissed me off, not because I felt I was being told I was wrong, but because of the principle of it. Based on my observations of our small agricultural community, I believed, and still do believe, that the work ethic of Hispanics is the same as, or greater than, any other segment of the local population. I immediately set out to prove a point: never judge people's work ethic or ambition by the color of their skin. Within a day or so, I hired a very nice Latina lady, and she was happy to start with us.

During the days that followed, I noticed my office manager becoming more and more agitated with me, and for the life of me, I couldn't figure out why. Finally, on a Monday morning, I told my wife, "I have to go in early because the office manager and I need to have a talk."

When I got to the office, there on my chair was a note from the office manager: "I can't work here anymore." That's all it said. I was hurt, but more than that, I was extremely disappointed. She was racially prejudiced, and I hadn't realized how profound her prejudice was until I found that resignation note on my chair.

Our prejudices damage our potential. As we discussed in the last chapter, some of our greatest accomplishments happen when we collaborate with others. If prejudice sets up a tent in your mind, your work with a team of diverse individuals becomes challenging, if not impossible.

Chuck your biases.

If you have difficulty grasping that idea, think of another saying from kindergarten: "Treat others the way you want to be treated." If you don't want someone to jump to conclusions about you, based on trivial facts—how you dress, how you look, what car you drive, your skin color, and so on—offer that person the same respect without prejudgment.

For those of you who appreciate biblical advice, it's right there in the Bible: "Judge not, that ye not be judged." Seek to be objective. Often, you'll find that upon closer inspection, you'll arrive at a much fairer decision.

Nothing good has ever come, or will ever come, from being prejudiced. Instead of focusing your energy on such destructive thoughts, retrain it on yourself in ways that will help you foster growth in your life and in your mind. In the next chapter, we'll discuss a lesson that will help cultivate that growth and success in your life.

CHAPTER 4

Have Tenacity and Strive to Persevere

When I think of tenacity and perseverance, the first person who comes to mind is my father. During the Korean War, he and his fellow marines were ambushed by the Chinese near the Chosin Reservoir. A harsh seventeen-day battle ensued—in freezing weather—during which the reservoir iced over, earning it its nickname, "Frozen Chosin."

Many people lost their lives during the ambush. Determined to survive, my father fought his way out under fire. After all, he had a fierce goal: to arrive home to his young, pregnant wife, safe and sound. As long as there was a breath left in him, he refused to quit. So survive he did. In fact, in the end, he was one of only two men from his company to walk out of that reservoir, but both his feet were frozen at the heel. He was sent for treatment at a navy hospital in California, and my mother was given base housing to be near him.

I've heard the story of my father and Frozen Chosin multiple times, and as a young boy, I already knew that in our house, quitting wasn't, and would never be, an option. Once you had started a task, you were fully expected to complete it; perseverance was an attribute valued above all others. Dad was the model and the master of this quality and his influence has served me well, helping shape who I am today, despite my self-esteem issues and doubts. So that's the next important life lesson I want to talk about: have tenacity and perseverance.

All creatures are meant to grow into greater versions of themselves. Think of butterflies. They transform from ugly, hairy caterpillars into creatures of beauty and splendor. Snakes continuously shed their skin, revealing a rejuvenated, healthier layer. The same is true of life. We start off as caterpillars, cozy in our own cocoons, but as we grow, we transform, leaving the cocoon behind to become the embodiment of something grander, more spectacular. Tenacity and perseverance are the secrets behind that transformation. By cultivating a mindset of ambition and motivation within yourself, you can push beyond your self-imposed limitations to become a better iteration of yourself than you were yesterday.

TIPS FOR MAKING IT HAPPEN

It all sounds great to say, but really, when you think about it, what does it take to persevere? How do you become a more driven, ambitious individual? There's more than one way to go about it.

One of those ways, I believe, is to become an avid learner, but I don't mean learning in the traditional sense. You don't have to be in a classroom setting to be taught by an instructor. Instead, read widely, listen intently, become a voracious observer of everything in the environment around and beyond you.

The best way I can explain it is through using the analogy of the shark and sea anemone. Both live in the ocean. Both need food, and both obtain it. The difference lies in the approach of each organism. The shark is constantly cruising, looking for a meal. It actively hunts and seeks. It has to keep water flowing over its gills, so it must move if it doesn't want to die. In the process, it doesn't wait for opportunities. Instead, it creates them.

The sea anemone, on the other hand, sits at the bottom of the ocean and waits for scraps of food, perhaps from the feeding shark, to drift down. It anticipates food rather than actively seeking it. There's no question about it: the anemone's strategy works, but the anemone is limited in what it receives and is completely dependent on its immediate environment, imprisoned in its current space and trapped in its strategy, while the shark roams freely, acquiring what it wants, as and when it pleases.

When you're seeking knowledge, be a shark, be intellectually hungry, eat ideas to grow strong in your intelligence. Sure, sometimes, you might consume a bad idea or misinformation, but at least you have an opportunity to purge it by seeking more accurate, better "food," instead of lying in wait, depending on chance for knowledge to come trickling down to you. Don't be a sea anemone. Self-serve. Don't just observe. Participate. Observation helps you gain understanding, and participation allows you to apply that understanding.

When you participate, the world offers the wonders of places, occupations, avocations, ideas, education, help, and training. Pursue the opportunities that bring your heart joy, the things that make you feel happy and fulfilled. Be passionate about opportunity. As the shark does, always look for your next target. Keep your eyes open and your ears peeled for new chances to help yourself grow and expand.

Another way to expand your abilities and persevere in your efforts is to seek multiple mentors in multiple disciplines. Be open to that mentoring. Learn from people who started as novices, as you did, but developed themselves to become reputed experts in their industries. The absolute best example I can give of this principle is a gentleman named Dr. John Kois.

About twenty-five years ago, I needed a mentor to help me take the next step in clinical dentistry. I had taken a couple of courses from John and knew he had a special talent. On the evening before I was to attend a study club meeting he was leading, I asked him to meet me and my wife. To my utter amazement and pleasure, he not only agreed to meet us but said he would come to the hotel where we were staying. Once he arrived and we got to talking, I plain out asked him if he would be my mentor. He asked me what that meant to me, and I told him I wanted to learn as much as I could from him, beyond what he taught in his courses. I told him I would do basic lab work for him or assist him at the chair. I would have volunteered to carry his briefcase just to be able to associate with him and absorb as much of his knowledge as possible. Without ceremony, he agreed and a relationship far beyond and of much greater value than just teacher-student began.

We are, ultimately, the sum of all the people who have influenced us and, for that matter, the sum of all the people who influenced them. Rarely do we actually create something that is completely original. Gaining knowledge by design is much better than absorbing it passively. The beauty of mentors is that they should give you candid feedback about your progress and your accomplishments.

I have had many other mentors throughout my life, including people who have filled voids in my formal education, and family mentors, such as my grandparents and parents and uncles and aunts, who have contributed untold hours of loving direction. Coaches often contribute to our development and well-being beyond what might be expected of a formal teacher. People in your chosen field or profession can also be inspiring mentors, and I have benefitted from many such people. Each of us is the focal point of knowledge and energy from all of the light bestowed on us through the ages by mentors and mentors of mentors. It becomes our responsibility, then, to become the conduit of our accumulated knowledge for the next generation. We are Lego-block beings constructed of all the blocks of those who have gone before, assembled by our own desire and will and opportunity.

Set aside self-pride but remain confident in realizing the fruits of your labor. That can be a tough balance to strike because people are often perceived to be arrogant when what they actually have is solid self-confidence.

Distinguishing between arrogance and confidence involves two major factors. They can be distinguished by data and opinion. To be sure, data and opinion can and do influence each other.

Here's the deal. Our opinions must stay flexible. If they become too rigid we stray from confidence to arrogance. After all, another term to describe an arrogant person is *opinionated*. What cannot be proven is usually a matter of opinion. You have to be careful, even diplomatic, about how you express opinions. There is nothing wrong with having an opinion, but be prepared to have others disagree and be prepared to change your opinion if new data is presented. Often, it is best to agree to disagree on such topics.

Religion is one of the most divisive topics and can breed some of the most destructive situations imaginable. Often arrogance on the part of one or both parties, groups, or populations leads to violence in the name of a supposedly peaceful practice. There is no way to gather definitive data to prove the main contention of most religions: the existence of a god. Even still, millions of people have been persecuted and killed by others professing to have a superior "knowledge" of a supreme being and who are intolerant of those who don't share the same beliefs.

Data represents those things that can be known, measured, calculated, and observed. If you try to refute data with opinion, the conversation will likely break down and become an emotional quagmire rather than a constructive discussion.

An example might be that of an odor. Even if two or a dozen people agree a certain odor exists, it becomes opinion as to whether it is a good or bad odor. What about music or art? Certainly, people can agree to hearing a sound (at a certain decibel level), but is it noise as opposed to music?

You must be your own judge. Remember that "people convinced against their will are of the same opinion still." You will have to decide if you are arrogant or confident, mushy or cocky.

Stand firm. Go with the facts, and declare what's true. Don't be afraid and back down because you start to second-guess yourself or because you're afraid of what people will think. Tenacity means pushing ahead, even when the going gets tough.

Finally, "Begin with the end in mind." Without knowing where you're going, you won't know how to map your journey. You won't know when you've reached your destination and when it's time to seek and set new goals, which we'll talk about more in depth a little later.

YOUR PURPOSE

Everyone should have a goal, a direction in life. Without purpose, life is like a lemon without zest. You have to know your calling. It's okay to flounder as you attempt to identify that calling, but to realize true growth, you have to find your true passion. Ask yourself why you're here. Find yourself on the map. I keep going back to the map example because it's the best way to describe how to discover yourself and your true direction in life. As I mentioned in chapter 1, to effectively use a map, you must know where you are and where you want to go.

In chapter 2, we also talked about the value of understanding your true north, your core values. Without getting too technical, I want to clarify that true north is different from north, also known as the magnetic north. (True north is near the North Pole and the magnetic north is above Canada.) I wanted to make that distinction clear to avoid confusion later, when we talk about orienting your map.

Getting back to the point, your true north, your core values, should guide you. Otherwise, you could make the wrong journey and end up somewhere that's in conflict with those values and beliefs, which will leave you dissatisfied.

This is a rehash of what we discussed earlier, but I want to delve a little deeper into core values in this chapter because they're really the heart of everything involving life's lessons, including tenacity. They determine *how* you persevere. Core values set the direction for your journey but don't necessarily dictate the end result. Rather, they show you how to *achieve* that end goal. Core values are the lines you paint in your mind as you work toward filling your life with color and purpose.

In my office, we have a poster displaying our six core values. I didn't decide on them on my own. We came up with them as a team, because when you're part of a team, you still have to work within a set of values. Otherwise, you could end up all over the map, ambling in different directions to achieve the same results or no definitive results. The end result may be the same for everyone, but the path each team member chooses to take could damage their relationships with the others. Values vary among individuals, which is why it's wise to come to an agreement on those values at the outset. Whether you're working in a team or on your own, lay down your map and find your true north, asking, "Which core principles can we agree never to stray from?" As Walter used to tell me, "Decide that with which you will not put up."

Answering this question will require introspection. You have to ask yourself which values challenge your threshold of tolerance. Which ones would you not compromise? Which values, if challenged, would stir you enough to make you belligerently defend them in the face of challenges?

Once you have your core values and map out your journey, you should feel a sense of peace. If you feel ill at ease, it probably means something's wrong. Either you've misidentified your core values or you've mapped your route incorrectly, or you're on the wrong journey.

I find calm in the storm as long as I'm progressing, I'm familiar with the vessel, and I know which direction I'm traveling in. I find peace in that confidence. I'm not at peace when I'm waiting for food to fall from the shark's mouth.

I used to be a pilot, so I'm accustomed to orienting maps, which is perhaps why I'm on this banter about maps and plot points and what not. Anyhow, I remember that when I was flying, I'd always rotate my chart to have the direction I was flying in sit at the top. If

I were flying south, south would be at the top. Having north (not to be confused with true north) on top wasn't important, unless, of course, that was the direction in which I was heading. Rather, the orientation of the map is what was important—that and knowing the obstacles in the way.

The orientation helped me stay focused on where I was headed *next*—not on my ultimate destination. Sometimes, before you make it to your ultimate destination, you need to arrive at several other points first, called way points. So it's important to focus on those first. You may call them mile markers or secondary goals; what they are called isn't important. You may travel from point A to point B, point B to point C, and point C to point D, before getting to point E, which is where you want to end up. Your journey may not always be a straight line, but that's okay. Focus on your next destination and the one after that, one stop at a time. Recognize when you're off track, reorient yourself, and make the corrections you need. It's all part of the course.

Once you orient your map, plot your destination, persevere until you land at your ultimate stop. The last step is about finishing and polishing, because, once you land, there's still a lot of opportunity to learn and progress beyond where you've landed. Perfect, buff, and polish, and keep going as long as you're alive and kicking because there's always room for improvement.

TENACITY TAKES DISCIPLINE

Beyond mapping and plotting, there's another really important element to being tenacious: being disciplined. In fact, the two go hand in hand. Discipline requires finishing a task even when it becomes challenging, inconvenient, or uncomfortable to complete.

You could be a reservoir of ambition, grit, and drive, but if you're not disciplined in your approach, if you're not committed to working on your craft constantly and consistently, then none of those traits matter; you won't see the results you're looking for.

Mathematically, we as human beings are the sum of the decisions we make, multiplied by our discipline.

As you might have guessed by now, I'm a man of analogies, and I've got another one for you. Think of tenacity as being the motor that powers a car and discipline as being you, the driver. No matter how fueled up your gas tank is, if you don't ever get behind the wheel and navigate that car toward your destination, you'll never get anywhere. The truth is, no one can drive a parked car. We can get behind the wheel and bounce on the seat like a three-year-old and twist the wheel and flip the blinker, but if the car is not moving, it cannot be driven. By the same token, even a car going backward can be driven, directed, and oriented. Tenacity is what moves our vehicle.

With discipline, even the smallest decisions can have grand results. By the same token, big decisions with little tenacity can have poor results.

The best example I can think of is marriage. When you decide to get married, you make a big decision about your life. If you don't have the willpower (tenacity) to nurture that marriage, to live up to your commitment or vows, then your lack of discipline can ruin your marriage and turn what could have been a decision with positive outcomes (a family, happiness, love) into one with negative outcomes (heartache, wasted efforts, divorce).

So remember, without discipline, decisions are the fodder of empty dreams.

THINK YOURSELF SUCCESSFUL

We've talked about why tenacity is important, how to put it to practice, the role core values play as you practice perseverance, and the significance of discipline in delivering you to your destination. Another crucial element in all this—in achieving your goals, in being dogged in the pursuit of your dreams—is your mindset. Fill your mind with the essential nutrients of knowledge, strategy, positivity, and wisdom because it's proven that we become what we think.

Growing up, I did a lot of thinking. My goal in high school was to graduate. My goal in college was to get accepted into dental school. In dental school, my goal was to graduate. In the military, my goal was to get out and start a private practice.

In fact, I was such a thinker and goal-setter that I had what I called a goal notebook. It housed my family goals, spiritual goals, and professional goals. I segmented my professional goals by year, brainstorming what I wanted to achieve in one year, two years, five years, and ten years. I thought it was a great way to break things down into smaller chunks, but then I stumbled into a pleasant but silly caveat: I had achieved my year ten goals by year three. I'd paid off my entire practice. Goals had always been the rudder and sail moving me forward, and now that I'd achieved this final one, I felt suddenly lost, disoriented. Where did I go from here?

I fell into a strange funk. I started wondering if this was all there is to life: going to work, drilling some teeth, coming home, playing with the kids, chasing the wife around the bedroom, and then going back to work to do it all over again.

In my melancholic state, my ex-wife and I started arguing and fighting, bickering about stupid things that didn't warrant a blow up. It got so bad that we ended up divorced, which was troublesome. I suppose I could be dramatic and say it was devastating, but it was certainly troublesome. I lost a small fortune in the divorce, but the silver lining in the entire mess was that it lit a fire under me, serving as an incentive for me to start setting goals again because, quite frankly, I had to buy my practice again. So I worked on resetting goals, reexamining what I was doing, and thinking about where I wanted to go. In the process, I found the woman I'm married to now. We've been married thirty years, so there's a happy ending there.

The lesson to learn from my ordeal is this: avoid drifting. Set the next objective as you move toward your current one. Don't ever be without a goal. Always stretch for higher horizons. Otherwise, you'll grow complacent, which is the worst kind of trap to fall into. Don't be content and don't ever mistakenly assume there's nothing more to live for. Seek new projects and hunt for goals or for something that will fulfill your life. The best way to achieve what you want is to set goals, making sure they are in harmony with your core values so you don't feel remorse when you finally achieve them. Be persistent, be tenacious. Don't give up.

FEEDING OTHER SHARKS

Being a strong shark with a voracious appetite is great, but remember there are still plenty of other hungry sharks roaming the waters. The secret to optimizing your achievements and feeling satisfied lies not only in your ability to feed yourself but also in your benevolence to take what you've gained in knowledge, competence, and wisdom through your tenacity and share it with other hungry sharks in the ocean. When you feed others, you expand your own strength of knowledge. So don't be selfish with that knowledge from fear that someone might benefit from it more than you did. You control the heights of your success. Share knowledge. Spread it. Teach it to others.

Over the years, I've realized that teaching others has been the greatest way for me to really engage myself in the learning process. As they say in Latin, "Qui docet discit," meaning he who teaches learns. Knowledge is strength, and the great thing about knowledge is that it attracts opportunity. As Louis Pasteur once said, "Chance favors the prepared mind." So sharpen your mind with knowledge and wisdom. Prepare it for great things to come, be persistent, be disciplined, and you'll see results.

In the next chapter, we take a cue from this idea of serving others to discuss another important lesson: protecting both yourself, and others, fiercely.

CHAPTER 5

Protect Others and Yourself Fiercely

O ne day, I was looking out my office window when a movement caught my eye. A young man was kneeling next to a car's tire, removing its hubcaps.

At first, I thought he was simply changing out a flat. Once he was through, I watched him glance around before he scooted back to the left rear wheel. That's when I realized he was stealing hubcaps!

I was enraged. I couldn't believe the man's audacity, even though the car being vandalized wasn't mine. I stormed out of my office. Just as I neared the exit, the owner of the car also caught a whiff of what was going on and scurried to his feet, livid. Together, in a cloud of rage, we marched outside and launched a verbal attack on the thief. He was flabbergasted to be caught red-handed, and we escorted him off the property, sans hubcaps, of course.

It wasn't until much later that I realized what the car's owner and I had placed in jeopardy with our display of bravado. We had, essentially, abandoned all regard for our personal safety, forsaking it for a few measly hubcaps.

That's not to say that what we did was a mistake. In principle, what the man was doing was undoubtedly wrong on every count, and we were right to speak up against it. However, it amazed me how easily we risk our lives for something as insignificant in value as hubcaps, only to step aside when things of greater value are snatched from beneath us, such as our ambitions.

It's a paradox. We'll risk life and limb to protect something as silly as a car's hubcaps, while at the same time letting people talk us out of our dreams, our values, and our hopes.

Defend your dreams. Defend your commitments. Defend your decisions, even in the face of disapproval from people who may mean well.

After my college advisor had planted in my brain that I had what it took to pursue something in the health profession, I had renewed aspirations, but because I was afraid my family would ridicule me for my dreams, I never shared them with them.

My grandfather tended nurseries and farms for a living. At that time, popular opinion assumed that someone from an agricultural family was limited in what they could aspire to. The dreams of the non-wealthy had an invisible ceiling.

It's true that my family didn't have a lot of money. Don't get me wrong. We weren't poor where it counted. (It is hard to be a fat kid, as I was, if there isn't enough to eat.) However, our lack of financial stability led people to assume that even if I had the grit to become a dentist, I wouldn't have the financial backing to follow through.

As this fledgling dream began to gain momentum, I accidentally let it slip one day to a family member. He stopped what he was doing, glared at me, and asked, "Who do you think you are? No one in our family has even been to college and you're going to college, and now you think you are going to be a doctor? Boy, that's rich."

There's one thing most people don't know about me: one surefire way to get me to do something is by telling me I can't. This person told me I couldn't go to dental school because I didn't have a way to pay for it. So began my quest to make sure that I *could* and I *would*.

The point here is that this person I hoped would be proud of me and support me in my ambitions was trying to extinguish the flame of hope within me, limit my progress, and dampen my motivation.

Unfortunately, he wasn't alone. He only said what others who knew my family's background were already thinking.

To be honest, they were right: my family didn't have the money to put me through dental school. However, everyone who doubted my dreams also underestimated my resourcefulness because as soon as I was accepted to dental school, I got to work applying for scholarships with the armed forces.

By some divine stroke of luck, I was accepted by all three branches of the services, all of which offered a full-ride scholarship, covering my tuition, fees, books, equipment, and a living stipend. The hardest decision I had to make was determining which branch to select.

My dream, my drive, my aspiration won out over the negativity projected toward me. That's what happens in most cases. If you stick to your guns, if you cling to that hope, if you don't let others down you, or allow them to tell you that you can't do something, there's not much that can stop you. You're your own greatest propeller and fiercest hindrance. Your success lies in your hands.

Yet before you're able to protect something—anything—you have to first understand that it's worth protecting. So that's what we'll talk about next.

REALIZE THE VALUE OF YOUR TREASURE

Think of something that's valuable to you. Maybe it's your car, your watch, your home, your family, your respect. Would you ever purposely let anyone harm those things? Would you let anyone steal them from you without putting up a ferocious fight?

Many people don't fight for themselves, because they fail to realize their own worth. The truth is that it's not until you believe something to be valuable that you'll find it worth protecting.

To protect yourself, you have to value yourself first. Appreciate who you are. Appreciate what you stand for. Appreciate the things you do for the people you love. Appreciate what you contribute to the world around you.

Once you realize your worth, set out to protect yourself with the same vigor and ferociousness you would anything else you value. Defend your dreams, your ambitions, and defend your values. Even defend your mind; build a protective shield around it. To do that means you should fill it with good thoughts, read, have mentors, invest in yourself.

Another way to protect yourself is by including among your associates people who have similar values. When you're around people who have shared beliefs and ideologies, it's less likely they'll steer you in a direction you don't agree with.

This brings us to another important point. Essentially, there are two categories of values: the internal and the tangible.

We must know who we are, what we are, what our values are, or else we risk letting things that are of less value displace those of greater value.

As individuals, we select which of those values means the most to us and make them a part of us. Many times, you'll find that several of these values are related. Integrity relates to honesty. Honesty relates to virtue, and virtuousness relates to ethics.

In any case, choose the specific values that mean the most to you. To test if they truly matter to you, ask yourself, "How vigorously would I fight people who challenge this value by doing XYZ?" For example, if respecting others is a value, you might ask yourself, "How vigorously would I fight people who challenge my value of respecting others by showing disrespect for a waiter or waitress, in front of me?" Your response to that statement should be a clear indicator of which values are truly significant for you.

The other way to identify values integral to you is by doing what someone once advised me: imagine yourself at your own funeral and think about what you'd want people to say about your character.

Each of us can think of at least a few things we'd like to be remembered for at the end of our journey. Maybe, for you, it's your kindness, your empathy, your wit, your generosity. Ask yourself why. Why is it important for people to know you as a family person? Why is it important to be known for your integrity? Dig deep to understand the *why*. Uncovering the answer to that will teach you so much more about yourself and your principles.

Once you identify the values that mean the most, don't ever transgress from them. If you do, you'll risk losing your integrity. Without integrity, no human being is human. Rather, have conviction in your core values and have the courage to fight for them. If you have that conviction, you'll find that courage often easily follows. As Winston Churchill once said, "Never give in, except to convictions of honor and good sense." Find your core values and then have the courage and integrity to stand up for them.

Most importantly, don't ever feel compelled to sacrifice your self-worth on the altar of compliance.

That's just a fancy way of saying that there are and will be times when we have to be independently strong to resist giving into social pressure and stand up for what we believe in. Don't sacrifice or suppress your opinions or beliefs to conform to those pressures just to appease others or to comply with their expectations.

It might be that your religious or political or personal beliefs are being challenged, but don't be persuaded against your intellectual will or core values to abandon something you uncompromisingly believe is important. That saying comes to mind again: "A man convinced against his will is of the same opinion still." So be true to your opinions and beliefs; don't just put up a facade of conformity when you know your opinions remain unaltered. Have the courage to fight, or at least respectfully agree to differ.

When I was in high school, there was a young man whose political views were in stark contrast to my own. In hindsight, perhaps, his views were more appropriate for the times, but in any case, he never once—not once—wavered from them. He endured all sorts of social pressure and peer pressure. People formed opinions about him and they judged him, yet no matter what resistance or ridicule he encountered, he never strayed from his beliefs. He stood firmly by them, never to be dissuaded.

Even today, I admire the integrity he had. By standing firm, he wasn't trying to draw attention to himself or gain notoriety; he was simply and absolutely committed to his core beliefs and did not comply with any social norms that conflicted with them.

I think he's an associate editor at *Rolling Stone* now. I'm sure his conviction and his confidence in who he was at his core are, in part, what helped him reach those heights. It's well deserved, and it's—I believe—what happens to people who stay true to themselves. They row ahead swiftly on the waters of life, never to be side-swept or shipwrecked.

So that's what I mean when I say don't sacrifice your worth on the altar of compliance. Stand firm in what you believe.

Once you know you're valuable enough to protect, and you start defending your core values, it's time to learn how to protect others.

LOOKING BEYOND OURSELVES
TO PROTECT OTHERS

We're all interconnected through our habitats, our environment, and our ideologies. Every action we take creates an effect on someone else. I believe we all have to contribute to our world because it's the right thing to do and because, even beyond that, what we feed into the world is what we get back. If you feed patience, you receive patience. If you feed love, you gain love.

As they say, you reap what you sow, which is why so much of this book is about giving back and not only doing right by yourself but by others as well. So once you learn to shield yourself from the bad, I believe it goes without saying that what comes next is to do the same for others.

For example, when my grandson decided he wanted to pursue a career in dentistry, his counselor asked him why he wanted to enter a "dying profession." Surely, he would be better off choosing a liberal arts degree and pursuing general education.

When my grandson relayed this message to me, I went completely berserk. With much effort, I finally regained my composure and sat down with him to do some research. Together, we were able to discover a handful of articles stating the contrary, including one from *US News* that ranked several specialties of dentistry and general dentistry in the top ten best jobs in the country.

Having suffered through many instances when people tried to drag me down, I wanted to make sure my grandson had the support he needed to surge toward his dreams unhindered. I will always support him and will walk shoulder-to-shoulder with him against any dream stealers he might encounter. As for his counselor, I suspect that after the education he received from my grandson, he'll be a little less presumptuous and assertive in stating his opinion as fact, going forward.

Protecting others doesn't mean just watching out for the people you love. It means being virtuous enough to stand up for anyone who needs protecting. For the longest time, I wasn't sure if I had it in me to be that virtuous.

When I was only a junior in high school, my cousin Bobby was killed in Vietnam. I was hung over in despair over his death, and I was angry.

At about the same time, an army lieutenant who was enraged at the loss of his men's lives, led a platoon into the village of My Lai, killing pretty much every man, woman, and child there. The news of this massacre was not exposed until a year or so later, when I was in basic training and saw that some army leaders—sergeants and such—didn't have a moral compass in terms of how to handle that type of situation. They supported the soldiers who had killed the men, women, and children in the village.

Yet I worried that I, too, wouldn't have the moral integrity to resist doing what I perceived to be wrong in a situation like that. For example, if someone were to threaten you with injury, or threaten to take your life if you didn't do something you believed to be morally wrong, would you have the guts to say, "No, I'm not shooting a four-year-old in the head, because that's completely against my core values. I can't, I won't, do that."

Would I really have the guts to stand up to these guys who were teaching me to obey orders?

I remember that when I started dating, just as I'd get ready to leave the house, my mother would always say, "Remember who you are. Decide what you won't do before you have to decide what *to* do." While she was talking about the choices I'd make in going out with these ladies, I think what she said applies to life in general. Think about how you'd like to react in certain situations before you're forced to react.

There did come a time in my life when I had to decide what to do—not under any grave circumstances—but it was a decision to be made nonetheless.

My wife and I were visiting Spain and staying in this hacienda, where I met Joe, a fellow American tourist. I hit it off immediately with Joe, who was about ten to fifteen years my junior. He had a slight but noticeable limp, which he informed me was from a knee injury that had cost him his candidacy for the NFL. His size and build gave credence to his claim. He was a giant, even to my six-feet-two-inches and 250 rather flabby pounds.

The men in our group were returning from an outing one evening to find that our wives, to accommodate the needs of our host, had agreed to move us into a different facility than the one we'd been staying at. The new place was the original hacienda of the ranch we were staying on and was older than the USA. The doorways in this dwelling, because it was built several centuries earlier, when people were much smaller, were considerably lower than doorways are today. They were only about six feet in height, meaning Joe and I had to duck to avoid knocking our heads.

As we were walking in, however, Joe forgot to duck and ended up whacking his head against the doorframe. Perhaps because of some earlier frustrations he'd experienced during the day, this made him disproportionately angry with the property manager, a sweet lady named Lucia. He began bellowing at her, spewing profanities as he towered over her.

I was stunned. "What the heck is going on? This isn't right," my mind screamed. Then a voice inside me asked, "So what are you going to do about it?"

Something inside me snapped. I stormed up to this guy and said, "Just a minute, Joe. You're my countryman and you're representing our country. So who the hell do you think you are treating anybody like this? You should be ashamed."

I was continuing this tirade to shame him when it registered that he could break me like a twig. I had gotten his attention enough that he'd fallen silent. When I was through, he made an attempt to physically intimidate me before he ducked his head and slunk into his room. His wife was much more of a lady than he was a gentleman and looked mortified.

That's the first time in my life when it struck me that I might actually have the integrity and courage to stand up against wrong, even if my personal safety was on the line. More telling, in this case, was that the other men and women in our group did not engage the big guy in any way. Since no one else protested, there was significant social pressure on me to ignore this man's abuse.

The cherry on top, for those of you who appreciate a happy ending, is that Joe left the next day, and the owner of the facility, whom we had not yet met, invited my wife and me to dine at his house as a token of his gratitude. His place was palatial, and for the record, it didn't have low ceilings or doorways. What it did have was a dining table that seemed to stretch on forever.

As we sat down, he gave me a gracious smile. "Lucia said that you were very kind to her yesterday," he said.

A little embarrassed, I replied, "Well, I'm not so sure that I was kind. I was ashamed of my countryman. He was totally out of line, and I couldn't let that pass."

"From now on," he said, "You are my guest."

I smiled. "Well, I appreciate that, but we've been your guest for the last three or four days now, and we've had a wonderful time. We couldn't possibly ask for anything more."

"No, no, no," he said. "You don't understand. Anything you want is yours. There is no charge for it."

I was pleasantly dumbfounded. The point is that when we stand up for what's right, sometimes good things happen, but even if they don't, just knowing that we stood up against wrong is in itself reward enough. For me, on that Spanish ranch, having that other part was pretty nice too!

So protect others whenever possible, but also respect their values. Don't be the person they need to be protected from. This leads me to another interesting point.

DON'T BE A CLAWING CRAB

Protecting others is important, but it's also just as important to make sure you're not the impediment to their success—or the person they need protection from.

I live on the West Coast. Often, we go crabbing, which is kind of fun. Our version of crabbing is similar to that of the TV show *The Deadliest Catch*, but on a less grand scale. We pull in our crab pots and dump them into the bottom of a small motor boat. The crabs start crawling around and we sift through them, throwing the ones that are babies or females back into the water and collecting the decent-sized males in the holding bucket.

What was really interesting was seeing the difference between having just one crab in the bucket versus having two or more. When we had just one, that little rascal would climb right out and pretty soon, he'd be back in the boat, scuttling around. Studying two or more crabs is what fascinated me because every time one of the crabs would reach up and start to pull himself out, the other(s) would claw him back in.

With one crab in the bucket, you need a cover to keep that little bugger in, but with two or more, there is no need, because they are each other's greatest obstacle to freedom.

Sometimes, we are like crabs in a bucket. We drag each other down the moment we get a whiff that others are making headway toward their dreams. We start attacking them to keep them down, because jealousy gets the best of us.

Protect yourself from crabs. Protect your goals, dreams, ideals, and core values, and just as importantly, don't be a crab.

In this and the previous chapter, we've talked a lot about serving yourself but also about serving others as you would yourself.

As I said earlier, we're all connected, so it's important we work together. That leads us to our next life lesson: be independent but understand the value of interdependence.

CHAPTER 6

Be Independent but Understand the Value of Interdependence

No man is an island,
Entire of itself,
Every man is a piece of the continent,
A part of the main.
If a clod be washed away by the sea,
Europe is the less.
As well as if a promontory were.
As well as if a manor of thy friend's
Or of thine own were:
Any man's death diminishes me,
Because I am involved in mankind,
And therefore never send to know for whom the bell tolls;
It tolls for thee.

John Donne

As babies, we can't walk, talk, or even sleep without the help of our parents. We're weak, fragile, powerless beings at this stage in our lives, completely dependent on someone else for our survival.

Fast forward about eighteen or twenty years, and you've got a job, you're cruising around town in your own car, you have your own place, you're paying your own bills. You're totally independent, no longer reliant on someone else for your well-being and livelihood.

Now comes the interesting part: we go from being dependent to independent to interdependent.

At work, you're collaborating with a diverse range of people while you work toward a common goal. Everything from school to home depends on teamwork and group efforts—from completing a deadline-driven project to making sure all the other team members are doing their share of sorting, washing, folding, and filing the laundry. Interdependence is telling of the level of maturity in a society or organization. The better people work together, the more mature an organization is. This is how mankind, over centuries, has achieved things that no single person could have ever achieved alone.

Dependence, independence, and interdependence, each has its place in our life—and they're all important in their own ways. Dependence is a small fragment of most people's life, happening toward the onset and end of life, in most cases. So independence and interdependence are what we'll focus on. They comprise the greatest chunk of our life.

THE FREEDOM OF INDEPENDENCE

One of the most celebrated events in any country's history is the day it gained its independence. Early on in life, we're taught that independence is good. When we're old enough to crawl, we're encouraged to walk, talk, write, read, and become self-sufficient. We're taught to be responsible for ourselves, to not depend on others to help us, to work independently, to use our own head to brainstorm solutions for problems.

In other words, we're pretty much forced to become an island unto ourselves. Independence is proven to cultivate self-esteem in kids and even adolescents. When we learn to do things on our own, depending solely on our abilities, we feel good. We gain self-confidence. These feelings of strength, self-confidence, and self-reliance are all great attributes to promote in children. They foster self-worth. They provide a reason for ambition and motivation: you know you can make anything happen if you work hard enough. There's no greater high than the feeling of independence.

In fact, from my earliest personal recollections, I have valued independence. I have had the vision and temperament of the typical "western loner" who could solve any problem and achieve anything on his own, and for the most part, I was successful.

I think my early multiple shortcomings—relatively low self-esteem and shyness—are what pushed me to solitude and, subsequently, independence. In any case, I began to find satisfaction in accomplishing and completing tasks solo.

At the age of eleven, I built a rowboat on my own, taking great pride in the hours of fun it afforded my cousins and me as we drifted up and down the creek behind my uncle's house.

Even when I took an interest in baseball, I was much more concerned with my batting average and fielding ability than with the overall success of the team.

I think that's how most kids think, when they're young. However, as you get older, further your education, join the job force, or even venture out into starting your own business, the world starts taking on new meaning.

You see that lives are much more intertwined than you once imagined. Behind your independence lies so much interdependence. After all, we're a social species.

THE GREATER POWER OF INTERDEPENDENCE

It's taken me a long time to realize that the truly great things that occur in humanity are the efforts of multiple people. From going to the moon to landing on Mars, it can't ever happen through the efforts of a single person. One man might have walked the moon, but it took hundreds more, working behind the scenes, to get him there. My personal progression to this understanding was a fascinating one for me.

High school football is when I began to realize the power of teamwork, yet I found I could still fuel my independent spirit through wrestling.

Football required eleven people to coordinate independently on the field in an interdependent manner. Wrestling, on the other hand, gave me the opportunity to succeed or fail against a single opponent, and receive personal recognition, independently of my team even if the team lost. For that reason, I loved wrestling more than I did football. Of course, looking back, I can see how juvenile that was.

When I graduated from dental school and entered the real world, I learned—the hard way—that building a business is not a one-person endeavor. In most cases, a businessperson has to lead and inspire cooperation among individuals, forming them into a cohesive group with a common purpose. That's what leads to financial and professional success.

Yet the concept of interdependence goes much deeper than sports teams or business ventures. It penetrates the very core of nature.

Animals, ants, and bees are interdependent instinctively. They only know the colony, the interdependent whole. Humans are the only beings that can willingly and knowingly arrive at a state of interdependence, understanding full well that there's greater achievement in that than in working independently.

My most critical experience with interdependence was when I was in the infantry. We were thrust into squads and platoons, and what I learned very quickly was this: if everyone didn't succeed, no one succeeded. During PT (physical training) tests, because I was one of the bigger guys and in decent shape at the time, I hung back to make sure that the last guys were able to complete the tasks. That's when I actually started to figure out that it wasn't just a question of saving your own butt; it was a question of getting everybody through.

When I moved past that and onto dental school, I found that dental business partnerships were extremely frowned upon. In fact, almost everyone I talked to at the time about setting up a practice said partnerships didn't work, because people always ended up venturing in different directions and couldn't agree on what they wanted out of the partnership.

The idea was you went to dental school, you graduated, and you started a one-person practice. That's what everybody did.

Little by little, the partnership idea began to gain popularity. Pretty soon, people saw the value in interdependence and then group practice. They started saying that having a partner was a good thing because you could split the overheads of the business between two people instead of one.

When you come together, the outcome is magnified. You're not just adding; you're also growing exponentially. As they say in the navy, "A rising tide lifts all ships." The rising tide can be a metaphor for ideas or cooperation, and when we put our ideas together and collaborate with one another, we can lift more than just our own ship; we lift everyone's. We all benefit.

That's why we should trust in interdependence. Count on other people. As I said earlier, trust and assume trust. We must take that risk of assumption and count on others, because, together, we can achieve more so long as our assumptions aren't proven wrong.

Even as we become interdependent, we have to respect core values. We must have shared values and beliefs that we work within and never deviate from. We have to be in agreement on those core values. Otherwise, we risk conflict and the breakdown of interdependency.

Going back to the ideas I expressed in chapter 4, you have to make sure that to work together, you lift the veil of prejudice. Once you do this, you open the doorways to connectivity, to interdependence, to greater good. With prejudices rooted firmly in our minds, that level of collaboration becomes impossible to attain, limiting our achievements.

LIFE: A WEB OF INDEPENDENCE AND INTERDEPENDENCE

When you're young and naïve, you may fool yourself into believing that you need only yourself to subsist.

The truth is that life is an intricately laced web of independence and interdependence. Without one or the other, the web loses its might, and the individual loses his balance.

In 2008, during the time I was experiencing issues with my heart valve, I went caribou hunting in the far reaches of northern Quebec. This was the start of an independent activity.

I took off through the tundra on that very first morning and spotted some caribou running up a little hill. I could clearly see where I thought they'd cross, so I decided to try and run ahead of them. (Don't ever do that. It doesn't work.) Ready to execute my plan, I had taken about ten steps when I began feeling faint. The world spun before me, and I lost consciousness. I was by myself in the tundra and not visible to others. Apparently, I remained unconscious for quite some time until, finally, I heard people calling for me. I could not see them, or they me.

With a great deal of effort, I was able to raise my hand and yell. Then I blacked out again. Luckily, that was enough for them to locate me and activate a system of interdependence. The person who found me called other people from his hunting group, and they decided to call for a helicopter to have me medevaced out. This effort required an entire network of people, equipment, and facilities to take me from the middle of nowhere into Kuujjuaq.

Kuujjuaq had a medical center. That's a lie. They had a first aid station. I was having a cardiac problem that they were not equipped to handle. So, again, there was reliance on interdependency and group effort to fly me to Montreal.

Montreal is where the interdependency fell apart completely. I ended up at McGill University, literally on the sidewalk, waiting to get into the emergency room, which was the first place I could truly be diagnosed.

I finally got a room, but it wasn't until about eight o'clock the next morning that the nurses came to take my blood pressure—and still nobody had gone through any diagnostic procedures with me. I decided I was getting nowhere fast, so I got up and pried the IV out.

"What are you doing?" the nurses asked.

"Leaving," I replied.

"Well, you can't leave!" they said, but I did, and just like that, I was back to being independent again.

Outside the hospital, I hailed a cab, went back to the hotel where I'd dumped my hunting gear just a couple of days before, rearranged my return flight home, and called my wife. Someone from Kuujjuaq had contacted her earlier to make her aware that I'd fallen unconscious. On the plane out of Montreal, I looked a sight. Just think about it. I'd been up in the weeds for several days. Nobody wanted to be in the seat next to me, and honestly, I didn't blame them nor did I want them there either.

When I finally landed in Spokane and disembarked, I spotted my wife right away. She looked right at me and then looked past me and around me. She kept doing that until I finally reached her and said, "I'm home!"

She did a double take. "You?" she exclaimed.

Honest to God, she didn't recognize me.

The bottom line here is that life is an integration of independence and interdependence. You can't live life being completely independent, nor can you be completely interdependent. Somewhere in the middle, there's a sweet spot between the two, and that's where most of us dwell.

So be independent but also interdependent. Share knowledge. Share resources. Share time. Be generous with it all. What helps others may, ultimately, come back to help you. This ties neatly into our next life lesson: the art of being generous.

CHAPTER 7

Be Generous

We make a living by what we get; we
make a life by what we give.

Winston Churchill

When my daughter Jill was a young dental assistant, her boss told her about a dentistry-related charitable opportunity in Nicaragua. Immediately, she signed up to go. The purpose of the event was to administer dental work to those less fortunate. At the last moment, however, Jill's boss's father became ill and Jill's boss couldn't go, so I was "recruited" to replace her.

The mission was divided into two phases. First, we went to the mountains and stayed in an orphanage and worked at government "health" facilities and schools. Jill and I witnessed excruciating poverty, and yet, these people were joyous and shared sustenance with our whole team. Contamination and filth seemed to be the order of the day in the "health care" facility, so we spent much of our first morning scrubbing the floors and walls with bleach. Then we began to work, feeling overwhelmed by the physical needs of these people. We couldn't keep up, despite setting up what amounted to an assembly (or disassembly) line for extractions of the most diseased teeth. The schools were actually much cleaner and, in them, we were able to convert class rooms into operatories by using the tables for treatment.

I brought small, inconsequential toys to give to the children we might treat. The response to these simple little gifts (fragile glider airplanes and butterflies) was to nearly create a riot of excitement and anticipation. I felt as Santa might have felt if he'd thrown a party for these kids.

We thought we'd seen it all as we left the mountains and journeyed back to Managua for the second phase of the mission. There, our group stayed in a new orphanage building that had not yet opened. We slept in clean dorm rooms, but each morning, we entered a world that we could never have imagined on this planet. I cannot describe the desperation and poverty we saw and smelled and heard.

The city of Managua is like any other city in creating vast tons of garbage that go to the city dump. Many of you may have had occasion to visit an open dump, where you've seen rats and seagulls picking through refuse for bits of food. Now imagine each of those creatures morphing into a human being who picks through the garbage for their next meal or for materials to build a shelter. This is what citizens were doing in the Managua dump city. It was a city of human refuse as well as the refuse of the citizens of Managua. This invisible population lived in indescribable, unimaginable squalor off the city's trash.

We saw a man whose legs had compound fractures and gangrene so severe that he was sure to die. We saw various stages of syphilis and even some dental disease. We saw hopelessness, fear, poverty, and every devastating condition possible. The temperatures were scorching and there was no air conditioning. We worked our best, doing what we could for children, adults, and the elderly, which mainly consisted of extracting teeth and offering antibiotics for as long as they lasted.

Despite the heart-wrenching poverty and dire circumstances around us, the experience was extraordinary, especially because it was an opportunity for Jill and me to bond over a common cause. For Jill, it was even more special because she was able to administer her first injection and extraction due to the fact that the law is somewhat lax in that part of the world compared to US law.

While this trip held great sentimental value in allowing us to forge a unique connection as we contributed a bit of our efforts to the world, it also helped us develop a strong sense of gratitude for each other and for the great things we were fortunate enough to have in our own lives.

Sometimes we need a wakeup call like that to realize there is a world beyond our own, where people aren't as fortunate, where men, women, and children are suffering, where there's pain, where sanitation is nonexistent, food is scarce, shelter is a blessing. We have to realize that while we're enjoying a warm bath, someone else is sweltering in the sun, praying for rain and water. While one of us is relishing lunch, another of us is dying of hunger. This paradox of life is real—and it takes place every single day in the world we live.

That's why our next lesson is so important: be generous.

That's a loaded statement because generosity means so many different things to so many different people. I think it's important to talk about what it is, but before that, let's explore the root of this tendency.

TRACING GENEROSITY AS A HUMAN TRAIT

I believe generosity is an inherent human instinct that supersedes our animal instincts of individual survival. Nearly every species of animal and insect—lions, wolves, elephants, bees, ants—is known to care for its young.

When it comes to helping outside the colony or herd or pack, humans are the only creatures I know of that have the self-awareness and understanding to knowingly and willingly accept the risk of personal loss, including injury or death, and transcend the instinct of individual welfare to help others, because generosity is a deep-seated part of our being.

Think about how we react when natural disasters or other forces of destruction wreak havoc on our world. Instead of focusing on just our well-being and safety, we pool together, pouring countless resources of money, energy, and time into saving, helping, and rebuilding the community at large. We support one another. I believe that's because we're genetically engineered to help others.

You'll never see a scrubbed-up, well-groomed child from a third-world country appear on an ad for poverty alleviation. You'll see children who look their filthiest, who haven't taken a shower in days, whose bones protrude through their skin, who have flies crawling across their forehead. Have you ever wondered why they don't clean those kids up? It's intentional. Research and studies prove that this sort of display tugs at some visceral part of us. It stirs sympathy within us. It makes us want to help, and I think that's because there's some subliminal realization that what we give today will somehow be returned to us in some form or fashion tomorrow.

We can trace this concept of reciprocation of generosity to our earliest history as hunters and gatherers. If someone found a bunch of berries, they'd keep enough for themselves but also share them with the rest of the group with the expectation that if others hunted something the next day and had an excess of it, they would return that kindness.

In his book *Influence: Science and Practice*, Robert Cialdini acknowledges this presence of reciprocation in our ancestors as an early human trait, making a strong argument about how it has influenced the cultural development of society. He says, "By obligating the recipient to an act of future repayment, the rule of reciprocation allows one person to give something to another with the confidence that it is not being lost. The mutually beneficial exchanges of our ancestors evolved into a sound interdependence among humans. As a result, people were (and are) trained from an early age to comply with the rule of reciprocity."[2]

Now let's contemplate what generosity actually means.

---

2   Robert B. Cialdini, *Influence: Science and Practice* (Boston: Allyn & Bacon, 2012).

GENEROSITY DEFINED

Generosity is giving freely of something you possess. Often when people think of being generous, they think of donating money. While that's a great way to practice generosity, it's certainly not the only way. One asset many of us have—and often overlook—is time. When we utilize our time in combination with our particular skills in life, we have an opportunity magnify the effect of our contribution. I think some of us discount the value of our time, whether it is shoveling mud out of our neighbor's front room after a flood or performing first aid at a car wreck.

Teachers have a unique opportunity when donating time as they often bring their teaching skills with them. This allows them to initiate a cascade of generosity. They can disperse knowledge by teaching someone how to read, write, or acquire some other proficiency, which can then be passed on to other individuals in a mode of generosity.

Similarly, mentors can offer time to students looking to specialize in something, for example, people working toward their GED or a career certification.

They say time is money, but I disagree. Time is more valuable than money, because money can always be re-earned, but time, once it's gone, vanishes forever. So offer yours freely but wisely. Invest it in places and efforts that will make a true difference to those who receive it, because once you give it, you're relinquishing a part of your life that will never return.

Recognize people's generosity if they offer you their time. They're giving you a priceless gift.

Say, however, that you're extremely busy and you don't have much time to spare. Maybe, you have wealth. You can choose to donate money to benefit practically any number of people: orphans, the underprivileged, battered women, the homeless, the disabled, babies—the list goes on. Organizations that serve these groups are always in need of monetary donations.

If you're limited in both time and wealth, think of other resources you could contribute. It might be that you could give freely of gently used items such as clothes and books, or you could give food once a month to your local homeless shelter. You could take an elderly neighbor to the grocery store.

The options are limitless. With generosity, there's no room for excuses. There's no place to say that you can't do anything at all for the community at large, or even for just a single person. Generosity requires only willingness and desire. Find what you can contribute, however large or small, and make a commitment to that contribution.

WHY GIVE?

To me, generosity is a moral imperative. It's a social obligation we must all fulfill because we each have something to contribute to make the world a better place in which to live. If we pool our talents, our time, our assets to make that happen, we're better human beings for it. We feel better about ourselves, and our society progresses, which means we progress, our families progress, our future generations progress.

Another reason to be generous is to give thanks. We each have blessings in our lives that we often take for granted: our health, home, family, food, water, clothes. We should count those blessings and be thankful for them, and the best way to practice gratitude is by giving, and helping others who aren't as fortunate.

A lot of what I'm saying may seem like common sense to most people, but sometimes, in our day-to-day obligations, the world around us fades into the backdrop, and we find just ourselves and our families at the center of our focus. We need to keep the power of generosity within us. We need to keep our focus broad and remember that we're part of a larger picture.

For those of you who are religious, you might practice generosity as part of your religious rites. I spent a lot of my early life closely attached to the dogma of organized religion. Over the years, I've become agnostic, but I often yearn for the comfort I had in "knowing" there was a god and being able to turn to that ultimate source for strength and guidance in prayer and meditation.

I still hear an inner voice, but have trouble attributing it to anything besides my own thoughts and prejudices and experiences and teachers. Yet as I look at my life and the blessings I've received, I have a sense that there is some vast, magnificent, benevolent power that smiles at our arrogance and folly and rejoices in our success in good works.

Somehow, someway, I feel I must pay tribute and homage to that universal power or, perhaps, being. I don't know how to do this except to try to do good to and for those around me. Doing the right thing is a direct acknowledgment of that universal power.

MY PERSONAL EXPERIENCES
WITH GENEROSITY

As I mentioned earlier, when you think of giving back, think of the resource you have the most of. Mine is dentistry. It's the one thing of which I have the most to give. As you now know, I have a strong military background. My dad was a war hero, and I was in the army and navy. Because that's such an intrinsic part of who I am, I've developed an affection for military veterans. The resource I'm able to draw on the most—dentistry—and the group I have a strong affinity toward—veterans—provide me with a way to practice generosity. One day, every quarter, my practice provides complimentary dental services to veterans.

This is particularly important because I've seen firsthand how veterans suffer from a lack of dental benefits. Many people, still in their prime, return from Afghanistan and other war zones scarred by battle and plagued by trauma. For these people, who have fought and risked their lives for our country, to have dental discomfort on top of all that simply because of a lack of funds is unjust and unnecessary—there are professionals like me who have the skills and resources to ameliorate their pain and eliminate at least one of their worries.

When I was starting in dentistry, the economy was crappy. My parents and grandparents suffered through the Great Depression, so they'd often cautioned and counseled me with wisdom about preparing for the future, including sticking money under the mattress.

I remember that when it came time to defend my choice of profession, I told people that even if the economy were to go to hell, there'd always be people with teeth problems. So I could always swap an extraction for a chicken to feed my family. There would always be an opportunity to barter dentistry, a thought that provides me a sense of security.

Luckily, I've never had to swap a cavity filling for my next meal. In fact, I've been quite fortunate, even compared to my parents and grandparents, which is why I think it's important I be thankful for my good fortune and pay it forward through my skills and knowledge. That's how the Free Dentistry Days event was born. I'm certainly not the first to offer such a service. There are many dentists who have similar programs, such as Smiles for Life, and it makes me proud to be a part of an industry where people believe in banding together to give back.

Our office team even received an award from Cathy McMorris Rodgers, the chairman of the House Republican Conference, for our efforts on behalf of these veterans. I mention this not to boast but to show that our passion is paying off, our efforts are appreciated, and we are making a difference enough to be recognized for our work.

Some principles from Free Dentistry Days apply routinely at my practice and not just for veterans. We have a rule that everyone at the office is aware of: we don't allow any individual to be in pain or danger at any time simply because that person can't pay for the treatment. No one who comes to our office is allowed to leave with a dental problem that we can fix. We care for all those who need dental treatment regardless of whether they're able to pay. It could be the town drunk or the mayor—whoever calls us with a problem. The only question we ask is "How soon can you get here?"

Aside from that, our practice has also been involved in the Relay for Life for over sixteen years. Each year, we provide breakfast for teams who stay at the track overnight. As you might know, ordinances usually apply when food handling is involved. At one of these events, some of the food vendors weren't very happy with us giving away what they had hoped to charge for. So one of them called the county health inspector in hopes of closing us down. As luck would have it, and, I believe, because we were out there, genuinely, to give and do good, we ended up passing with flying colors and even added another certificate to our collection of service accolades.

When I look back at my life, I realize that a lot of my beliefs about generosity and giving back stem from what I witnessed growing up.

For twenty years, my dad worked as a bookkeeper for a man named Charles Anderson, who owned a furniture store. Dad was amazing with numbers and he was a loyal employee. However, because he was in and out of hospitals during his recovery from war wounds, he often missed work. However, in all the years he was employed, Mr. Anderson never missed delivering Dad's paycheck. He kept the paychecks coming even when my dad was in a psychiatric ward. I remember that one summer, I did harvest work for my grandfather, and we took what I had made and stowed it away in a cigar box because Mom was afraid that Mr. Anderson's goodwill might not extend forever—but it did. Never once did he let us down, and he taught me at a very young age about the power of generosity, setting the very high standards I wanted to live up to. In my eyes, he achieved a level of goodwill and generosity that few people ever achieve.

I can say the same for Dad. Just as Mr. Anderson's generosity had no bounds, neither did his. It was a time of civil unrest in Portland, Oregon, and there were a lot of riots. Mr. Anderson owned the largest furniture store around, and one day, a strong gust of wind shattered many of the store's large plate windows. I remember my dad grabbing his deer rifle and setting out. He sat in that store, amid broken glass, hugging that rifle to his chest to protect Mr. Anderson's furniture against looting, without ever being asked to do so.

I saw this play of generosity unfold in front of my very own eyes. Mr. Anderson was dedicated to Dad, and Dad to Mr. Anderson. Their generosity toward each other had no bounds. It was so copious that it was difficult to overlook. So their generosity became a living, breathing lesson to me at a young age. Their actions taught me beyond what words ever could. "Charlie" was an example of what I wanted to become, and to this day, I strive to be like him.

GENEROSITY IS CONTAGIOUS

When you instill a little bit of good in the universe, it usually multiplies and expands before eventually finding its way back to you. The same can be said of generosity. A little bit goes a long way, and usually, a simple act of generosity can catch on like a contagion.

A few years ago, at one of our Free Dentistry Days events, I treated a gentleman who had served in the army. Although we'd made it clear we wouldn't take payments, he insisted on paying something. Our front desk person flatly refused his tender, moving him to tears of gratitude. Choked up, he finally managed, "I want to help too," and he presented us with a check that was substantially more than our services would have cost him had he come in on a regular treatment day. "Please use this money to offset some of your costs," he said. We were all proud to accept his contribution and honor his generosity to the cause.

We have another patient who writes a check for expenses incurred during Veteran's Day events. He always insists, saying that because he's a farmer and busy tending to his land, he doesn't get much of a chance to help out. He sees our Veteran's Day event as his chance to do good and offer his contribution.

Both these gentlemen are proof that goodness is contagious. Sometimes, one person is all it takes to spread generosity, to light inspiration within others. Be that person, the initiator.

There's another really interesting lesson hiding in here that I should share: I've never been able to give something without somehow receiving something in return. It may not be in the exact same shape or form of my own contribution, but I've realized the more good I give, the more good I receive.

If you look around, you'll find that this is, generally, true. Even extremely wealthy people, such as Warren Buffet, Bill Gates, and Oprah, give, not because they have tons of money, I think, but because they receive something back. Sometimes it's definable and tangible and sometimes it's not, but in some way, form, or fashion, the universe returns a gift to you.

My final lesson on generosity, before we move onto the next chapter, is what Anne Frank once said: "No one has ever become poor by giving." I agree. You can't give yourself into poverty. It's not possible to donate so much that you eventually grow poor because of your propensity to give. I believe there's a power or a force that for everything good you put in this world, you get something back. In fact, if you believe that, as I do, you'll see that kind of selfishness as generosity.

My grandfather, Grandpa Leitz, once said, "He who never does more than he is paid for will never be paid for more than he does." His words have always reverberated through my mind because they speak so well of the repayment of giving. The more good you do, the more you are repaid for your good. Anything you donate with your heart will come back to you for the better.

In the next chapter, we talk about life's decisions and figuring out how to do what's right at any given point.

CHAPTER 8

Do the Right Thing Using the Information You Have

In a world where death is the hunter, my
friend, there is no time for regrets or doubts.
There is only time for decisions.

Carlos Castaneda, *Journey to Ixtlan*

T his is a story I've told a thousand times, even though I
lived it only once. My dad was a real-life war hero. He and
his comrade were the only ones out of two hundred men
who walked out alive from a conflict in the Korean War, traveling
from Inchon to the Chosin Reservoir, and shooting his way back

down to the coast. I'm sure that upon his return, he was euphoric to have survived. After all, he had an expectant wife waiting at home. However, then came survivor's guilt, and his mental health began to go downhill. By the time I was fourteen, he'd spent about a half to a third of those childhood years of mine in VA hospitals.

In the meantime, Mom and I did the best we could on our own, working and tending to the house. I'd grown up around animals, but I was most attached to one dog in particular, Sheppy. Sheppy was a tiny mutt with a lot of shepherd dog in him, hence his name. At the time, I was socially inept, so I didn't have many friends in school, and the few I did have were outcasts like me. So Sheppy filled a big emotional void in me.

Unfortunately, while Dad was still in recovery, Sheppy fell deathly ill. He was lethargic and had lost his appetite. Because we'd looked after so many different animals, my mother and I believed Sheppy to be beyond treatment. Unfortunately, we didn't have the money for a veterinarian, but we were pretty certain any veterinarian who'd see him would likely suggest euthanasia.

For an entire week, all I'd do was go to work and come home to stroke a suffering Sheppy. He was clearly in discomfort, and we felt completely helpless.

Then, one day, when we couldn't watch his misery any longer, my mom came to me, a look of despair in her eyes and a .22 rifle in her hands. Taking a deep steadying breath, she said, "Sheppy's suffering, and you're the man of the house now. So we've got to do what we've got to do." With that, she handed me the rifle.

I was devastated. We both were.

Because it was the early '60s, and we lived inside the city limits, we didn't want the sound of gunshots to raise questions. So we went to my grandfather's farm about sixteen miles out of town.

I remember Mom putting me, Sheppy, and that stupid rifle into her little white 1962 Bel Air with its ugly red interior. I hated that car. I hated being there that day, Sheppy in my lap, his heart racing against my palm. I kept wishing, thinking, hoping that he would just pass away before we got to grandpa's farm so I wouldn't have to live that moment.

When we finally got there, Mom couldn't even bear to watch. Her face was creased in anguish. "Why don't you go on and take Sheppy down the hill there," she said.

I did, but it took me a long time to do it. He was finally out of his pain, I knew, but that didn't make me feel much better. After a while of staring off into the vast openness, I finally gathered the strength to dig him a little grave. I came back feeling as if a rock was pressed against my heart, and Mom and I had a good cry together. It's tough for a fourteen-year-old to break down like that, but at that time, I didn't care.

This is still a tough story for me to tell, one of the toughest, but it's an important one, because, sometimes, life requires us to do the right things—even if they're painfully difficult—based on the information we have on hand at the time. That's the lesson of this chapter.

DOING RIGHT . . .

Doing what's right can be subjective because what's right for one person may not necessarily be right for another. So how do you determine what's right and what's not? This is where core values again come into play.

As you make decisions in life, you'll have to reference that true north: your core values. These core values, as we've established, draw the boundaries within which you live your life. They're the boundaries within which you should aim to make all your life decisions.

When you step outside their bounds is when you're doing wrong. As long as you're within those bounds, you can proceed with confidence, knowing that what you're doing is correct, based on your beliefs, ethics, and morals.

That's why it's imperative to know your core values so that you can make decisions within those etched margins.

Then there's that second part to this lesson:

... WITH WHAT YOU KNOW AT THE TIME

I've learned that what you believe to be "the right thing" can change, based on what you learn over time.

What may have seemed right yesterday may not appear that way today because today you learned a new detail that influences your opinion.

Hypothetically speaking, I could have chosen to become a veterinarian instead of a dentist, in which case I might have recognized Sheppy's symptoms to be curable.

In those instances, it's easy to become overwhelmed with guilt or remorse. It's easy to grow resentful, sad, and upset about doing what you thought was right at the time, but living life that way is unrealistic and will only yield innumerable regrets. It's entirely possible, probably guaranteed, that you may look back later and see a different solution to a problem.

That's why the second part of our lesson is so important: do the right thing *with the information you have on hand at that time.* If, later, additional information is presented that invalidates your earlier decision, you can be sorry you didn't have the information earlier and you may even be sorry for the outcome but don't regret making a decision that was grounded in good faith based on what you knew *at the time.*

As I said earlier, hindsight is always twenty-twenty. Understand that when you're in the midst of making a decision, you aren't looking through the goggles of hindsight. You're looking through the lens of immediacy. You will probably make mistakes with your decisions, but it's impossible to make a decision based on what you don't know, so don't be too harsh on yourself.

For years, I tried to live by the mantra of "Do the right thing." Later, when I discovered a new detail or fact that made me believe I had done the opposite of the right thing, I made myself miserable: *I could have, would have, should have...* It wasn't until much later in life that I realized I was being unfair to myself. None of us has a crystal ball. No one can guarantee the future, let alone all of today's intrigue and innuendo, but decisions must still be made, and life must go on.

People will likely judge you along the way, putting even more pressure on you. Shame on them.

After reading about Sheppy, some people may believe my mother to be evil. (I'd beat the crap out of them if they were to say that! Just joking!) She might be criticized for dealing with the problem the way she did: by handing a fourteen-year-old the problem.

However, she and I made a decision based on our core values: we would always consider the pain of others before our own. Doing what we did to Sheppy wasn't for our benefit. In fact, on many accounts, it would have been far simpler for me to watch him pass naturally than to take him out of his misery, living with that memory the rest of my life. Our core values wouldn't allow that. It was far too selfish to simply sit and wait and watch him suffer more and more with each passing day. At the time, based on our experience with animals and considering that we weren't even sure if we'd be able to make the next mortgage payment, let alone pay a veterinarian, we did what we believed to be best. In the end, it was heartbreakingly difficult, so much so that this story is permanently etched into my memory, finding its way into this book even half a century later.

No one ever said doing the right thing is easy. Remain true to your core values, accept sorrow but avoid regret.

Another example of a difficult decision is firing someone. You might have solid grounds for letting an employee go, only to discover something, later on, that would have changed your mind about firing that person. It's natural at a time like that to think, *Darn! If only I'd known. I would have done it differently."* Again, we can't measure the success or failure of our decisions by information we didn't have at the time the decision needed to be made.

The only decisions we can rightfully regret are those we don't make or that we make poorly because of haste or ignorance.

In my adult life, one of the most difficult decisions I had to make was getting divorced. My wife and I had suffered through a lot of turmoil in our relationship. By the time things spiraled beyond repair, my eldest son was eleven, his brother was eight, and my youngest was six.

After years of bickering had effectively hacked away our relationship, I was aware of the exact moment when the proverbial axe connected with the final piece of timber keeping our marriage upright.

I was at work when I got such an unexpected phone call from the governor's secretary. I thought someone was playing a joke. She asked if I had a few moments to speak with the governor. At this time, I was thirty-five and had been working in my dental practice for about five years.

A moment later, the governor, Booth Gardner, came to the phone. "Dr. Laizure. Your name has come up, and I'd like to ask you to be on the state board of dental examiners. Would you please consider that?" he said.

"Are you sure you have the right person?" I asked, at a complete loss for words.

"Absolutely," he confirmed.

At this point I could not have been more dazed than if I had been sucker-punched with a two by four. "Well, in that case, sure. Count me in," I said, resisting the urge to pinch myself and not fully knowing what I had gotten into.

Despite being new at my profession, by most standards, I was, technically, considered a successful dentist. I had a big mortgage, a big house, and all the good things in life, and this call was another peg on my board of accomplishments. I won't lie. I was ecstatic, proud even. This was one of the highlights of my career, after all. I walked, maybe even strutted, into the house, feeling great. I found my wife at the sink, where she was busy preparing dinner, and my son was seated at the dining room table, doing homework. Finding him doing homework was probably one of the more remarkable events of a remarkable day.

I cleared my throat. "Well, I got a phone call from the governor's office today," I said.

I was anticipating some excitement, some cheer, some curiosity. After all, this was the highest recognition and honor I felt I could have received at this stage of my career. I'd been appointed to the state board of dental examiners, of all places, which, by the way, is hated by all dentists unless, of course, they're asked to join the board.

When she didn't respond, I added more detail: "I got a phone call from the governor's office, and I've been asked to be on the state board of dental examiners."

Still no excitement. To be fair, I don't know what state of mind she was in, but she looked at me almost as though she were looking through me. "Oh, wow!" she said. "You're going to be gone. That means you're going to take off again this weekend. Okay."

I was dumbstruck, not really knowing how to reply.

However, my son seemed to have sensed my previous excitement and said, "What does *that* mean, Daddy?"

I felt my excitement bubbling again. After all, every dad wants to be a hero to his son, and I was overjoyed to explain that his dad was about to embark on something really cool and special. Before I could begin to explain it all, my wife spun to face him and said, "It means your father has to go to Seattle to hobnob with the high mucky-mucks because now he thinks he's one of them too."

The pain and humiliation that knifed through me at that moment is almost indescribable. I went from an emotional high to feeling as if someone had just cut my legs off at the hips in front of my son. I was ashamed, heartbroken, and sad all at once at the look of puzzlement and confusion on my son's guileless face. That's when I knew I'd witnessed the final nail being driven into the coffin of our marriage.

After much discussion, my wife and I decided we had to take what we knew of our relationship and make the right decision in the interest of our kids. We decided it was better for them to be part of a fractured family than to be in a stressful, artificially sustained environment.

Thirty years after our divorce, and after a harsh battle with diabetes, my ex-wife passed away in 2016.

Her death led to an onslaught of remorse, particularly for my daughter, whose relationship with her mother had progressively gone from good to bad to worse to terrible until she felt almost antagonistic toward her. After my ex-wife's death, my daughter would often say, "I should have done this. I could have done that."

It was during these times that I would sit her down and try to explain that there was no way she could have known that her mother would pass the way she did. She had not even been aware of many of the circumstances her mother had faced, because she'd never shared them with my daughter.

One day, some months after her mother's death, my daughter gave me two totes full of photographs and memorabilia that my ex-wife had left behind. "No one ever told me about our family's history," she said, her eyes misting over.

I opened the totes to find a familiar assortment of photo albums and scrapbooks my ex-wife had done a terrific job of compiling. They were chockfull of our family histories and various segments of our lives. She'd included memories of our four years in dental school, and our four years in the navy, all events that had occurred before my daughter's time. Neither I nor, apparently, my ex-wife had ever shared our experiences of these memories with her.

She continued, "When I looked at these things, it was like looking into someone else's life. I really don't want them."

So I ended up with these two totes of material, plus a journal of my ex-wife.

One Sunday afternoon, curiosity got the better of me. I started to glance at some of that material, and I began to see a different perspective unfold: her perspective.

The journal was, quite literally, a translation of my life through someone else's viewpoint. It was strange to see how things went from my perspective to her different one. It was even more interesting to see how she had distorted my motivations and actions, for I saw them very differently from what she believed them to be. Neither of us was wrong, just different in how we viewed the same things.

Going through her journal that day, I was able to see more clearly why she'd made some of the decisions she had. Although I didn't agree with them, and still don't, the point is that based on the knowledge she had at the time, she, too, made decisions she thought were right.

I remember that when we were still married, I often wondered why she said one thing but seemed to do something else. Why did she act like that? I didn't understand her behavior at the time, but as I read her journal, in the light of an additional thirty years of personal experience, I was able to understand why she had acted the way she did, based on what she perceived to be true.

There comes a time when we all are forced to make painful decisions. Sometimes you'll look back and understand that, maybe, you could have done things differently or treated situations differently. The lesson to be learned is that, in looking back, you should have the wisdom to understand you can only do the best with what you have at the time. It's impossible for any of us to be omniscient enough to make perfect decisions throughout life. If we do, we'll only set ourselves up for disappointment and failure.

In the next chapter, we discuss the last and final lesson of this book: the power of not quitting.

CHAPTER 9

Don't Quit

By the time I became a teenager, I was used to feeling inadequate. The words, *big, fat, dumb* still echoed through my mind.

Then, in my freshman year of high school, something incredible happened. We had a PE challenge called the Man Lift and Carry, where each of us had to partner with someone approximately the same height and weight and hoist that person on our backs for a half mile.

Nobody in my class was my size, but there was this big guy—we'll call him Jerry Finkle—who was in sophomore class, one grade above me. So we were partnered up.

The day of the challenge, I was petrified. What if I failed again? This was not a noncompetitive challenge for the class but an individual challenge for each student.

I lifted Jerry onto my back, not without a struggle, I'll admit. Carrying him around was no easy task. Every muscle in my body was screaming with exertion, but something in my mind screamed louder, "Don't quit! You don't have to be first, but you cannot quit."

Jerry, on the other hand? Let's just say he wasn't what I'd call "highly motivated" or committed to the task. We hadn't made it two hundred yards when he started moaning and whimpering that his legs were hurting. Mind you, *I* was carrying *him*.

Finally, when I couldn't stand his blubbering any longer, I looked over my shoulder at him and said, "Jerry, we're doing this and we're going to finish it. Even if I have to throw you down, roll you and kick the living crap out of you to the finish line."

Luckily, that shut him up.

When his turn came to carry me, the whining and moaning started again. "I want to quit," Jerry mewled. His face had turned the color of a hot chili pepper.

"You can quit when you fall flat on your face with me on your back," I said.

The two of us completed that challenge, and in the end, even good ol' Jerry was pleased, albeit more than a little sore, I'm sure.

That event transformed me. It was the start of a new mantra in my life: Don't quit. You might get knocked down, but you must rise.

This thinking changed my approach to tasks and to life in general.

There's no greater proof of the impact that event had on me than the fact that even fifty years later, I still remember Jerry Finkle's name (which isn't Jerry Finkle) even though the only interaction I ever had with him was carrying him around that damned track, cussing at him (which, I'm really good at, by the way) and, maybe, beating up on him a bit when we played on the football team together.

The truth is that quitting is easy. Anyone can do it, but it takes a true champion to finish what was started.

Sometimes, giving up seems to be the only option, but it's only an option if you allow it to be one. Pump yourself up, especially when the thought of defeat seduces you.

One positive experience resulting from your doggedness will transform your mindset. One win will forever light a flame of hope within you.

My story's the perfect example. From the get go, the odds weren't in my favor. I was dyslexic, had confidence issues, was an outcast, and was overweight. Because of my insecurities and all the forces working against me, I even had issues with social integration.

Giving up would have been all too easy. I could have just retreated into my shell and resigned myself to a lifetime of defeat. I didn't, because I'm not a quitter and I don't want to be known as one. I'm the guy who likes to finish the things he starts.

When I think back to a few examples from my life, following that Man Lift and Carry event, I can identify the spirit of dogged ambition in almost everything I started.

For instance, after my counselor had planted in my mind the idea of pursuing a health profession career, there was no stopping me. His words made my self-confidence sprout. I found that was all I really needed.

Once I had finished the majority of required courses, I was accepted into dental school after only three years of college instead of the typical four. Normally, students had their BS degree in hand before entering dental school. For me, it was the other way around.

When I graduated from dental school, I had my doctorate (DMD) but still no BS degree, and that made me feel incomplete.

So I transferred my dental school credit hours back to Portland State, where I had started my undergraduate studies. Although that university accepted quite a few of my hours, I still needed eight more in the field of arts and letters to graduate. The reason for this was because they didn't transfer hours I had earned in dental school casting gold crowns using the lost wax technique, which is the same procedure sculptors use when casting wax models of their sculptures. I felt that was adequate to qualify as credit hours, coming from the same state system of higher education, however, Portland State didn't see it that way.

I thought, *Well, that's BS.*

I know it didn't really matter whether I had my BS degree in hand or not. I'd already accomplished what I'd set out to do: graduate from dental school and get my DMD. Yet I couldn't leave this task half finished, no matter how trivial that might seem. I had to finish what I'd started.

I ended up taking a course on the history of philosophy and logic and got those final dratted credit hours to graduate.

The course was completely useless. It didn't do much to contribute to my future career, but I took it because I wanted to feel I'd completed what I set out to achieve.

When I talk about not quitting, I'm talking about not only weighty matters such as getting an education but also tasks as simple as mowing the lawn but not getting that last tricky strip of grass in the corner, or drying the dishes but forgetting to dry the silverware too. I believe each task should be executed to completion, because anything less would be the same as giving up halfway.

When it comes to not quitting, two steps will help you keep going.

#1: BELIEVE YOU CAN DO IT

Once you start a task, you have to believe you have what it takes to complete it.

Before I applied to dental school, I didn't ask anyone. I just did what I thought was right and sent in my application. At the time, I no longer had the help of my prized counselor, Dr. Klein, since I'd changed my major. I acquired a new counselor, whom we'll call Dr. Russell.

If Dr. Russell had been my counselor all along, I probably would never have become a dentist. The moment he found out I'd applied, he immediately started berating me for shortcutting the process and wasting my $10 (or some nominal fee) for the application fee, which was a significant sum of money at the time. Further, he assured me that without his recommendation there was little chance I would be accepted.

I remember looking him in the eye and saying, "I think my wife and I can sacrifice a dinner at McDonald's and a movie, sir, but I do appreciate your concern, and I'm willing to take what comes."

Shortly after my meeting with him, I got called in for an oral panel interview at the dental school. I was flabbergasted. After my conversation with Dr. Russell, I was a little nervous about the interview, even going as far as to squander an entire eight dollars (which was a lot more money back then) on a new shirt. My wife came along with me and stayed in the car for moral support.

When I walked in, three interviewers were waiting for me. These were bright, intelligent minds, and I'm sure they probably knew I was wetting my pants as I sat down in front of them, although I made every effort to hide my anxiety.

Before we'd really had a chance to get started, or even acclimated to one another, two of the three interviewers started bickering over some inconsequential point that had nothing to do with me or the interview. It was so weird.

The argument swallowed up most of our time and grew heated. Voices were raised, and even though they weren't directed at me, I remember wondering what the hell was going on.

Our interview time drew to a close, and the head honcho (who was the only sane one in the bunch because he didn't get involved in the argument) sighed, cleared his throat, and managed, "Well, Mr. Laizure, we've taken a lot of time to…err…ask you some questions. Do you have any you'd like to ask us?"

The other two interviewers still appeared agitated and flustered, and the head guy looked as if he were one blink away from cardiac arrest.

Being my straightforward self, I looked him square in the eyes and asked him the only question I could think of, "Am I gonna be part of next year's class or not?"

I don't think they'd been asked that question before, because he kind of fell back in his chair and blinked his eyes as if I'd socked him in the forehead. "We'll get back to you in a couple days," he finally managed.

I thanked him and left him to the company of the other two.

As I trudged down to my car, I was pretty sure I'd bombed it.

I found my wife bouncing up and down in the passenger seat. "How'd it go? You'll actually get to go to dental school?!"

I gave her a lopsided smile and sighed. "Well, honey. There's always next year."

I honestly thought I was toast. Plus, I'd wasted eight bucks on a doggone shirt.

To my sheer surprise, only two days later, I got my letter of acceptance into dental school with the stipulation that I complete organic chemistry prior to enrolling.

Again, another flame of hope burned bright within me, prodding me forward, reinforcing the wisdom of always believing in myself, no matter what anyone else believed, because life doesn't always play by the rules; it doesn't always follow the same trajectory. The fact that a thousand students got their BS before their DMD didn't guarantee that would happen every time. Sometimes life surprises us, as it did me.

If you set out to do something, anything, don't quit short of doing it, just because you don't have enough confidence in yourself. Trust your gut when it tells you to do something. Learn to take chances. Learn to take a leap of faith, especially when that faith is being invested back in you.

The naysayers and the preachers tell you why you were wrong to take a chance, but so long as you believe in yourself, don't stop.

The second step, in some ways, piggybacks off the first.

#2: TRUST IN YOURSELF

Previously, we talked about trusting others, but I think it's equally, if not more, important to trust yourself. If anyone can get you through life's hurdles, it's you.

I've had to rebuild my practice four times.

When I first started, I was already setting one-, two-, five- and ten-year goals in what I called my goal notebook. The first goal my wife and I set together was moving to Walla Walla, where I purchased my practice in 1979.

Because I was still in the navy at the time, I didn't actually begin practicing until two years later, in 1981. Then something crazy happened. That damned mountain near us, Mount St. Helens, blew up.

Walla Walla is downwind from the mountain and fell under the southern edge of the ash cloud. That's when it started—this enormous outpouring of unsolicited advice from neighbors, friends, acquaintances, and even strangers at the grocery store.

Some told me to stay in the navy.

Some told me to move someplace else.

Still others advised me to throw in the towel and abandon dentistry entirely.

It's easy to get vacuumed into a cloud of pessimism and doubt. It's easy to allow your own apprehensions to swallow you whole, but I couldn't and wouldn't let that happen. I wasn't giving up, and I knew I had to trust in only myself to make this dream of practicing dentistry a reality.

In July 1981, I finally opened the doors to my practice.

In the first six months, my revenue doubled what I'd anticipated in my goal book. I had an incredible team that worked really well together. We started with just me, a receptionist, and an assistant. After the six-month mark, we'd expanded to one more assistant and a hygienist. By the three-year mark, I'd achieved my ten-year goal of paying off the practice.

There will be moments when you'll have to make tough decisions. You can't trust anyone except yourself to achieve what you want. Rely on yourself, and only yourself, to achieve your dreams.

Don't quit because someone else tells you to or thinks you won't be able to do something.

Trust in your abilities, in your skill, in your intelligence, in your willpower. Trust in you, and the results will most definitely follow.

STARTING OVER

After I paid off my practice is when I fell into that strange lull I mentioned previously. In 1986, five years after I'd started my practice, my wife and I filed for divorce, and because of the divorce settlement, I had to start all over.

I was remarried in 1988, and my current wife, Donna, and I had to start our lives from scratch.

Luckily, it didn't take too excruciatingly long to build things back up. By 1999 we'd taken the practice to a whole new level, quadrupling its revenue and even buying another practice and integrating it with the first. Then I brought an associate onboard. She did a wonderful job, and because I worked closely with her and saw what she could do clinically, I trusted her and we formed a partnership. Unfortunately, the partnership only lasted four months (this goes back to our lesson on assuming trust and how that can go awry sometimes). I never realized until then that a failed partnership could be as professionally destructive as a divorce. After the partnership dissolved, I had to start all over again, essentially. I rebuilt the practice and bought the last of six partners out of the building, which meant I now owned the whole facility. In 2003, I did a major remodel that cost me a million dollars. Just a year after that, I entered a whole new venture as part of my goals: I launched a teaching center under the guidance and mentorship of Doctor John Kois.

However, as you might have gathered from your own experiences, if not through my stories, life always throws a curveball at you when everything seems to be sailing smoothly.

The year 2008 was when I started experiencing heart issues, making the medical professionals wonder whether or not I'd survive.

An agonizing fifteen months later, they finally cracked me open and crawled inside my chest, taking out this piece and replacing it with that one, as you would do with an old Chevy. I woke up in the ICU, after the surgery, to find a physician sitting in the corner, reading something. It's never a good sign when you wake up in the ICU to find a physician in the room.

I blinked a bit, and he noticed me. "Oh, you're awake. Good," he said. He probably saw the uncertainty etched on my face, because he continued, "You shouldn't worry that I'm here. There was a little leak, and I just wanted to stick around in case we had to open you back up again."

"Great," I said.

Luckily, there was no leak. Turned out he was a pretty good seamster—and I hurt like hell.

By some overpowering sense of ambition (or stupidity—I'll let you decide), I managed to miss only eight days at the clinic. By the ninth day, I was digging in mouths again and drilling teeth.

The lesson to learn from my experiences is this: no one can steal your education, your drive, or your experience from you. Sure, there's no magic switch that can rewind time so you can start again. In my case, having my health and my knowledge to help me rebuild my future was the next best thing to having my youth returned. That's much better than not having any hope or alternative.

There's always a silver lining to every dark cloud. Sometimes you just have to squint really hard to see it.

I was able to rebuild my practice with absolutely zero thought of quitting. Starting over just became another item to check off in my goal notebook, another objective to work toward. If anything, it provided an opportunity to not become complacent. Because it's such important advice, I'll repeat what Churchill once said, "Never give in—never, never, never, never, in nothing great or small, large or petty, never give in except to convictions of honor and good sense. Never yield to force; never yield to the apparently overwhelming might of the enemy." I've always loved that quote. It aligns well with my own beliefs. As long as you're living, every day is a day to be lived to the fullest. Make the most of every moment, every opportunity, every new venture and adventure. Whatever you do, don't quit. When you start a task, finish it. This level of discipline will help you scale life's greatest mountains and seemingly insurmountable obstacles. With grit and perseverance, you can achieve anything you want. Nothing is impossible.

Having fought in Korea at the Frozen Chosin, my father often quoted one of that war's generals, Major General Chesty Puller, who declared: "Retreat hell! We're attacking in a different direction!"

That's what you should live by. If life throws hurdles at you in one direction, change direction, but attack back. Change your tactic of attack. Duck, shoot back, hide, but don't ever give up. Never give up.

I learned from my dad the value of barreling forward in life. If he could face an entire army at a frozen reservoir in a foreign land

and make it out alive without once thinking of giving up, I damn well have no excuse.

Today, I'm more experienced, more educated, more sagacious, and a little older, but it's all for the better. At least I can live life knowing I gave it my all.

Conclusion

When I was in the navy on active duty, my wife and kids and I lived in a duplex on the base in Hawaii. Ironically, on the other side of the duplex, lived another military family that was virtually a mirror-image of our own. The couple was about the same age as my wife and I were, and they had two boys, who were also about the same age as our sons.

Our familial makeup couldn't have been more similar. It was a bit strange but kind of interesting, too, living next to people who were so much like us. It was almost like staring at our own reflections from the other side of the firewall.

However, even though we were similar in most ways, there was one way in particular in which we were starkly different.

The military makes great noise about saying it cares for the medical and dental needs of family members. The truth is that those needs are usually considered second fiddle to those of military personnel. This means that at the end of the day, there's usually little, if any, time or resources left to treat dependents of military personnel.

There's a popular comment in the military that if the navy really wanted you to have a family, it would've packed one in your sea bag. So although the service personnel's medical and dental needs were taken care of, the dental needs of dependents were generally ignored.

Because I was a dentist, I was able to find a way around this hurdle by bringing my wife and kids in for free fluoride treatments and cleaning. As long as I worked on them myself during off hours, no one said anything, and the truth is, apart from their routine cleanings, my family didn't need any treatment.

In fact, in the four years we were on that base, my family had zero cavities.

That's where the other family differed drastically.

They had constant dental emergencies. Many times, they'd have to rush to the civilian "market" and pay high civilian fees charged to people who don't have insurance.

Why was that? What was so different about our families that caused the other family to need treatment when my family never did? We ate the same food, drank the same water, were approximately the same age, and lived in the same environment. In fact, the father in the other family probably had a master's in engineering and, as far as I could tell, had management and leadership qualities far better than mine, since he was qualified to operate a nuclear submarine. His wife also appeared to be intelligent.

So what was the difference?

Perhaps the answer to that question is obvious: knowledge. However, knowledge also involves the skill and ability to apply it.

Our neighbors on the base didn't have the knowledge to prevent the dental problems they were having, so they had to get remedial treatment. More importantly, they didn't have the skill to apply any knowledge they might have had to treat their family, as I could.

Knowledge is what benefited my family and the lack of a specific area of knowledge was their failing.

While the husband was a powerful man, very intelligent and authoritative enough to be trusted to command a nuclear submarine, his lack of knowledge in dentistry caused his family to suffer, economically and physically, which goes to prove that knowledge is the most important type of power because it provides choice and opportunity.

We're at the end of this book. I've lent you my goggles of hindsight to look at where you might be standing when you're my age. I hope I've covered some of the lessons you'll learn along the way about things you should do and others you should avoid.

You now have my knowledge, my hindsight, but I hope you also have something greater: the ability to apply that knowledge.

If you start to implement these lessons at a young age, you'll see the benefits throughout your life.

You can be more productive, live a more fulfilling life, offer more to the people around you, find more joy, and share the gifts of experience with others, or you can sit back and live life passively, letting things happen to you.

I'm sixty-seven, an age when companies won't sell me life insurance because they don't think I can live another ten years for them to break even on their investment in me.

The way I see it—so long as I'm alive, so long as you're alive—every day is a day to be lived.

To get that sense of fulfillment, you must not only live for yourself but also for those around you. Protect them, and if you can't protect them, at least don't jeopardize them.

With knowledge, we can prevent many of life's problems. With knowledge, we have a much better chance of restoring or repairing our errors.

If you keep these experiences, observations, and life lessons firmly in mind and start at a young age, you'll see the benefits throughout your life. It's never too late to start. Sometimes all you need is a course correction.

While you're out there implementing these lessons, remember this: Life is a fleeting journey and we all end up in the same place. The joy is in the journey. It's up to you to find it.

Printed in the USA
CPSIA information can be obtained
at www.ICGtesting.com
JSHW012038140824
68134JS00033B/3131